I0492396

THE CRYPTO NOVICE

THE HANDBOOK FOR THE CRYPTOCURRENCY BEGINNER

COLIN E. OLIVA

CONTENTS

INTRODUCTION

So, my view's quite clear. I believe cryptocurrencies, Bitcoin is the first example, I believe they're going to change the world.
– Richard Brown

This project originated from trying to learn about cryptocurrency. I, like everyone else, heard about cryptocurrency at work and from other people in conversations. I had my reservations, I thought it was all a trend or a scam of some sort, all these ideas and thoughts in ignorance. When I started digging deeper into the subject I realized what a huge potential this market had. I realized that it was in fact, a valid market with valid innovation that solves many of the world's problems. I found that this innovation could have the ability to change the landscape of the world's economy. Finally, how this could potentially be a huge wealth transfer to the people who got in early enough. I read about people who were early adopters who made millions out of small investments over the period of a couple of years. This excited me, these types of occurrences are rare, and no one should expect to make millions overnight.

Yet we are still at the beginning of the massive market explosion.

I started researching the subject, I got in deep. I had so much information flowing through my mind that I had to start writing it down to keep track of what I was learning. I decided to start a blog for beginners like me who would want to know more about this opportunity before making an investment decision. I picked a subject then would start writing, time after time my articles became so long that I would have had to break them down into two or three posts. That's when I decided I would write this handbook instead. I hope you enjoy it and learn something from it, it comes from my heart to yours in the hopes of helping people make good and knowledgeable investment decisions.

So, let's dig in, why are people so excited about this new market?

"I think the internet is going to be one of the major forces for reducing the role of government. The one thing that's missing but that will soon be developed is a reliable e-cash." – Professor Milton Friedman

"Bitcoin is evil." – Paul Krugman

"If you care about liberty, the nonaggression principle, or economic freedom in, general, you should do

everything you can to use Bitcoin as often as possible in your daily life." – Roger Ver aka "Bitcoin Jesus"

"Bitcoin is a very exciting development, it might lead to a world currency. I think over the next decade it will grow to become one of the most important ways to pay for things and transfer assets." – Kim Dotcom

"We don't really know how this coin is created. You can't have a functional money without a basic transparency. Unless you are addicted to volatile trading for the sake of trading, stay away from the Bitcoin. Thankfully its plunge will be a salutary caution to most folks." – Steve Forbes

"Bitcoin is the beginning of something great: a currency without a government, something necessary and imperative." – Nassim Taleb

"Bitcoin gives us, for the first time, a way for one Internet user to transfer a unique piece of digital property to another Internet user, such that the transfer is guaranteed to be safe and secure, everyone knows that the transfer has taken place, and nobody can challenge the legitimacy of the transfer. The consequences of this breakthrough are hard to overstate." – Marc Andreessen

"**Virtual Currencies may hold long–term promise, particularly if the innovations promote a faster, more secure and more efficient payment system.**"
– Ben Bernanke

"**Bitcoin promises to take at least some of that power away from governments and hand it to people. That alone augurs significant political, cultural, and economic clashes.**" **– Paul Vigna**

As you can see, Cryptocurrency is a very polarizing subject. On this matter, there are people who have taken the time to research the blockchain and cryptocurrency. People who are developers and as such familiar with the subject. There are early adopters who saw the potential early on and believed, who are now millionaires. There are also people who are too used to; or benefit too much from the current system to see a different point of view. To see the huge potential this new market has. This technology could usher in a new way of thinking. The blockchain and cryptocurrency, in general, are a game changer, the entire world economy could change from the advances in this sphere.

There are investors and early adopters, people and organizations who are jumping into this market with both feet. Reputable organizations, such as UPS,

FedEx, Disney, Amazon, and others who are investing in or creating their own blockchain technology. Wait, I thought we were talking about cryptocurrency? We are, we will explore this further along, for now just know that blockchain is the technology behind cryptocurrency. In this book, you will learn all about the origins of cryptocurrency, why it is such a departure from normal currency and the current economy. We will discuss what the blockchain is, why it's such a big deal, why and how it will change many industries. We will investigate if cryptocurrency can replace the current system of paper currency. We will dive into conducting research and learning more about cryptocurrency. I will introduce you to some of the cryptocurrencies which I believe have the greatest potential for growth. How to start investing in this sphere and we will discuss some of the most commonly used strategies.

The Early Adopters

Early adopters are people who worked on projects like Bitcoin, programmers and computer techs who found out about this market early on, had the ability to look at the code and got behind it. Seed money investors who started funding projects and learned how monumental this opportunity really is. People who work in the computer industry who know how to read the code and found the programs interesting or discovered an opportunity and got in on the ground floor. Then there are just regular people who are tech savvy or early adopters of any new technology who got in early and got lucky.

The point is these people got in early and made millions, but it is not too late to be an early adopter. As good as Bitcoin is at solving some of the problems with paper currency it does not solve them all. It also has introduced many more problems, these problems need to be solved, which is why there are so many different cryptocurrencies now. That being the case we are still at the very early stages of this new market, the opportunity to make money in this domain is still available.

As this new field grows and matures it will shake out all the bad hands. This will allow the good platforms and currencies grow. There are many growing pains in new markets, some created by charlatans who see an easy opportunity to make money, others are just products that do not have viability. As the market matures it will correct itself, the products with no viability will disappear quickly and the charlatans will go away even quicker. A new market presents many opportunities to make money, sometimes a lot of money. The key is to know how to research so that your money goes to the companies or currencies which will be standing tall at the other side of the tunnel.

Misconceptions about Cryptocurrency

I also want to dispel some of the misconceptions that have developed about the cryptocurrency market. One of the most popular misconceptions is that it is too late to invest, the market has already come and gone. In the first chapter, we will compare the current cryptocurrency market to the market during the dotcom bubble. In Chapter 2, The History of Currency, we will see how cryptocurrency is not a passing fad, and why it is here to stay.

Further misconceptions are that it is difficult to invest in cryptocurrency and that it is not a worthwhile passive investment. In chapters 3 and 4, we will learn how to create a system for passive investing or active trading, laying a good foundation for your money to grow. It is difficult to get into the market, there is no way around that, you are changing your whole mentality from trusting others to safeguard your money to being completely in charge of your own wealth. This is difficult and requires careful attention. That said, in chapters 7 and 8 I will break down, step by step how to get into the markets, and how to safeguard your money.

With this book you will learn how to get started investing in cryptocurrency, and how to safeguard your money. You will learn how to control your own finances without having to rely on a third party or forced to put your money in a bank. You will gain confidence in cryptocurrency knowing you have a good foundation to rely upon to build wealth in this new space. You will learn how to educate yourself and become a more refined investor. Finally, you will learn step by step how to buy your first cryptocurrency, and how to safeguard it.

The hope is that this book will educate the public about cryptocurrency, the markets, and how to invest in them. The goal is to attract more of the public to come invest in this new market. I want my readers to get into the market now, before the rush begins, to capture a big portion of the gains that will come when mass adoption takes place. Mass adoption will take place in this market, I intend to prove why it will happen. In order to capture the greatest gains, the best place to be is invested in the market before mass adoption.

CHAPTER I

THE CRYPTO NOVICE

Bitcoin was created to serve a highly political intent, a free and uncensored network where all can participate with equal access.

– Amir Taaki

First, let me introduce myself, I am a just a regular guy who doesn't know much about anything. I know, stop reading now...right? I say that because I want my readers to know that I will be truthful in all that I do and say in this series. I do not have any experience in programming, nor am I a financial wizard. This book is not meant to be an end all be all resource for investment advice. This is for those, who like me, are interested in learning more about Cryptocurrency and Investing. I have a military background, and I have a degree in Finance. I have a basic understanding of how the markets work but I am by no means an expert.

Listening to people at work, the news, and hearing on social media about Bitcoin and Cryptocurrency I developed an interest and I started studying up on it.

At first, I was very skeptical, I thought that Bitcoin was what the unlawful used as money. I thought it was how gamblers, extortionists, and other criminals laundered their money. Where unscrupulous people would go to conduct their heinous business. The more I researched, the deeper I went I realized that the opposite was true. The crypto community is full of people who are just like me and of like mind. People who distrust the current system, who believe the game is rigged to benefit the top one percent. People who want to help other people take control of their lives, their wealth, and their freedom. To be truly free from the controlling overlords of our world. People with dreams of creating a system where we can all be winners, or at least have the chance to be.

I wanted to share what I had learned and learn some more along the way. In this series you, the readers, whether newbies or cryptocurrency holders will be able to take a journey with me in learning all we can about the crypto world. I have some very useful and powerful information that I would like to share with those who are interested. You will learn all about the history of currency and trade in general, what the blockchain is, all about Bitcoin and Ethereum, what Ripple is and why it's a big deal. We will discuss Initial Coin Offerings (ICO), and new systems and technologies that are coming out that could change the game. We will also discuss some other ways of getting into the crypto world via different maybe safer avenues, and many other topics along the way, as we learn more we can dig deeper into this new and exciting market.

Disclaimer

Spend each day trying to be a little wiser than you were when you woke up."
– Charlie Munger

First a disclaimer, or maybe just advice. As I have already mentioned, I am not an expert. I hope that the readers will never just take my advice and run head first into an investment they may not fully understand. Please, please, please do your own research. Do not invest one red cent until you understand where it is going and how it will give you returns. The reason I am writing this book is that, although I believe crypto will eventually change the financial world, it is a bubble and in any market bubble there will be scummy people who will try to scam innocent people out of their money. So, do your own research and make sure you understand your investment.

Second, never and I repeat never invest more money than you are comfortable with losing. Any investment comes with risk, but the high volatility in the crypto-currency market makes it difficult to time the market appropriately to ensure you will make money on your investment. Trust me there is plenty of money to be made in this market and hopefully you and I both will make a good share of it. I just want to ensure that we are doing it the smart way, the right way, and hopefully not get burned.

I have always wanted to help people, I am the type that takes care of others. When I first started research-ing the cryptocurrency space I couldn't find anything, the information was spread out over multiple websites. It was hard to keep track of the information, it was hard to organize my thoughts. I wanted to create a product that would make it easy for people to start their research. Everything you needed to know in one place to ensure that people trying to learn can. The hope is that people can get into the market in an easy and quick manner.

Just in Time

You can't stop things like Bitcoin. It will be everywhere, and the world will have to readjust. World governments will have to readjust

– John McAfee

There is nothing like being fashionably late to an engagement only to realize the open bar closed five minutes before you got there. No worries about that happening in the cryptocurrency markets, it is very early on in this space. The crypto markets react in extreme ways to every piece of news that comes out, whether it be positive or negative. This is a sign that the market is very new and immature. In chart 1-1 below you can see the market for Amazon when it was very new and immature. The volatility, reacting to every piece of news, is rampant in the early days. We see it again in Yahoo Inc, chart 2-1, volume spikes during the bubble which causes volatility in the price. As you can see, after the period of extreme volatility when the market matures and stabilizes there is a long run where the prices stabilize, and the market grows.

Chart 1-1 Amazon[1]

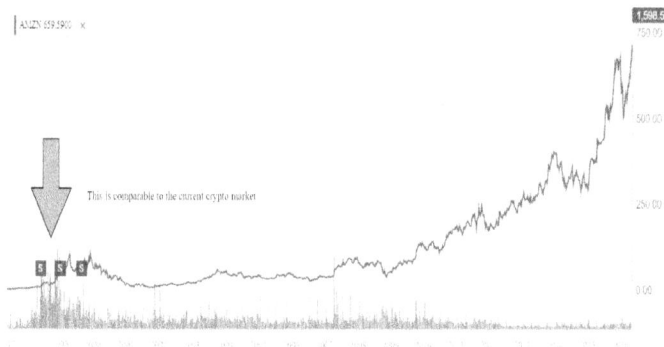

Chart 2-1 Yahoo Inc[2]

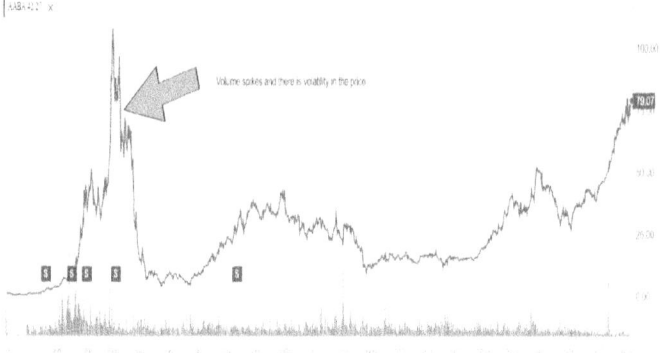

Institutional investors are starting to dip their toes ever so carefully into the crypto world. The market will mature and stabilize as regulation starts coming into the market, this will allow for mass adoption, which is the catalyst to the massive gains. The third chart 3-1 shows the current market situation for cryptocurrency, it looks very similar to the early days of Amazon and Yahoo Inc during the dotcom bubble.

Chart 3-1 BTC/USD[3]

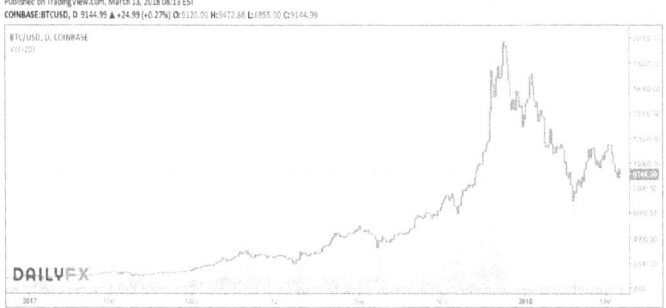

As you can see the chart for Bitcoin looks very similar to that of Amazon and Yahoo Inc very early on in the dotcom boom. You can see the spikes in volume and relationally the volatility in the price. When regulation comes into the market, whether government-forced or community (self) regulation, this will mature the market and shake out all the bad apples. Once the market matures we will see the long period of stability seen in the Amazon chart. It is imperative we, as investors, get into the market now before the market matures. We would enjoy the long run-up in price. For traders, extreme price volatility makes for amazing opportunities. They can ride the price hikes and short sell the dips. For them, the best time to get in is now.

We also see some differences between the Amazon and the Yahoo charts. Amazon's chart shows a long run up to its current price, a long period of stability and incredible gains laid out over the period of 16 years. On the other hand, we see Yahoo, which although still showing gains in the same period did not skyrocket like Amazon has. This is due to the management of the company. Amazon's management did an excellent job of nurturing the budding company, finding its identity and growing the profits and by default its share price. Meanwhile, Yahoo struggled to find its identity, struggled to create streams of income, and at times was just unlucky. At times Yahoo aggressively pursued other companies to find profits, other times was too inactive in their pursuit of good companies. Some of the businesses they bought turned out to be unfruitful, and some contribute a great deal to their bottom line. Yahoo struggled for many years and that results in a less successful share price. The lesson to learn here is that even good companies can struggle due to misman-agement, it is important to know who is behind the curtain.

For those who cannot read charts, the volume is indicated by the vertical red and green lines at the bottom of the graph. Red means there were more sell orders than buy orders, and green means more buy orders than sell orders. The line graph tracks the price movement. Volume affects price, meaning that when there are more sell orders (red line) then supply is going up which makes the price go down. Conversely, if there are more buy orders (green line) it means demand is going up which makes the price go up. This is the basic law of markets, the law of supply and demand. Demand goes up and prices go up, meaning supply is going down. Scarcity makes prices go up. Conversely, if supply is up, meaning demand is down the price goes down, the market is flooded with product. The volatility is seen in the wild ups and downs of the price graph. Volatility is bad, volume is good, as the market matures, and volatility decreases the volume will increase as more people will feel comfortable entering the market.

Traditionally, the biggest gains happen when the public starts to pour their money in. Early adopters and institutional investors can move the market, but once the market starts moving in the right direction the biggest sector of the population starts getting involved, the public. When the public gets involved in the market that's when the biggest gains are seen. Institutional investors carry a lot of weight, and by weight, I mean money, but it does not compare to the masses of the public. Institutional investors also have a fiduciary responsibility to their customers or shareholders to invest in a safe manner, so they diversify. This means that they may be in many different sectors to balance out their portfolio. Public investors, in general, don't worry about portfolio theory, or diversification. They see something they like, and they buy it. Some make money, others aren't so lucky.

As we can see, the cryptocurrency market is acting in a normal fashion for a new market. Speculation is creating price volatility; the market is reacting to any news with wild price swings. There are still some bad investments caused by the lack of regulation. There are scams and/or useless investments in the market. When the market matures, through self or imposed regulation, the stability will attract more investors making now the perfect time to get into this sector. We see that it is not too late, the cryptocurrency market is at the perfect stage for investors to take advantage of a long run-up in price.

CHAPTER 2

HISTORY OF CURRENCY

An investment in knowledge pays the best interest.
–Benjamin Franklin

In ancient times the market is where people went to trade goods and services, and to socialize. They traded these goods and services for other goods and services in a barter system. The inherent problem with the barter system is how to determine value for different items. For example, if I gave you some knowledge on how to care for your cattle and as a result, your herd gets healthier, grows bigger, and produces better for you how much meat or milk from said herd is that worth to you. An easier example, say I am a cobbler and you have a fruit farm, how many shoes do I need to trade for a basket of fruit, is it 1 shoe, a pair, multiple pairs, the values are relational to the products or services. Now imagine trying to determine the relational value between hundreds or thousands of products and services. It becomes near impossible, the markets for the products cannot grow, and the market, in general, becomes stagnant.

Currency provides intermediary value to the markets. Using currency, the market has an item that has a known value and can be used to purchase and sell products and services. Prices can be set for products and services based on the predetermined value of the currency. This allows markets to grow as the currency becomes the "gas" in the system. The first iterations of money first appeared in ancient Egypt and Mesopotamia in the form of gold bars, which still needed to be weighed to determine value. About 2,500 B.C. a large trade market in Elba, modern Syria, is established based on gold and silver. Before long, ornaments worn on the body such as rings and necklaces became a form of portable currency a tradition which lives on to this day. Currency in the form of gold and silver introduces some major problems. First, it can be easily stolen, this is important to us as it is a problem that persists to the modern day with paper currency. Next gold and silver are bulky, heavy, and awkward to ferry around. For traders in ancient times, they would have to dedicate resources just to carry their currency.

Around 1100 B.C. the Chinese introduce coinage, coins are in the form of a circle with a hole in the middle, so the coins can be stung on a rope. The first minted coins are introduced in Lydia, now western Turkey. Around 600 B.C. Lydia creates the first minted currency coin which is made of electrum. Electrum is a naturally occurring alloy of gold and silver. The coins were stamped with different images to denominate different values. The introduction of currency grows the Lydian markets and advances international trade. This made Lydia a powerful and fruitful city-state, prosperity continued until it fell to the strength of the Persian Empire. The Persian Empire adopted the use of coins and spread the practice throughout the ancient world. Alexander the Great conquered the Persian Empire and spread coinage even further. In Rome, bronze coins are used and are valued in terms of sheep and cattle. Numismatics, the study or collection of coins, is practiced to this day.

Attempting to fix the theft problem, gold and silver were stored in temples for safeguarding by the temple keepers. This raised another problem, as the currency sat in the temple vaults it wasn't being used by the people interacting in the markets. Loan certificates from temple priests began appearing in the 18th century B.C. in Babylon, giving birth to the concept of banking. Banking activities advanced in Greece and

Rome as financial transactions are introduced. Public entrepreneurs and temples take deposits, make loans, offer currency exchanges, and even test and weight coins for value and purity. The banking networks grow like wildfire throughout the ancient landscape. Now merchants can take a loan out in one city and take credit on the same loan in another city thereby not having to carry a large number of coins to transact in different markets. The Roman Empire spreads the coin-based economy and banking principles throughout Europe.

The first iteration of paper money comes from China in the 10th century A.D. Marco Polo was so awed by the practice that he wrote: *"the Emperor of China makes so many notes each year that he could buy the whole treasure of the world, though it costs him nothing"*. Unwittingly, in his comments, Marco Polo described one of the greatest problems with paper money. By 1350, continued note printing had depleted the Chinese notes to almost no value. Chinese paper money continued for several hundred years, yet the rampant overprinting continually led to runaway inflation and debasing of value. The Chinese eventually returned to coinage and relied on these as currency until the 19th century.

Paper currency makes its appearance in Europe in 1661 when Johan Palmstruch establishes the

Stockholms Banco, a private bank with strong ties to the Swedish government. The bank issues notes (banknotes) that could be exchanged for a stated amount of dalers; dalers are large copper plates used as the Swedish currency at the time. The bank would take deposits in dalers and provide a proof of credit to the customers. The practice became popular and the bank found itself with large amounts of dalers. Naturally, Palmstruch started issuing loans based on the dalers on deposit. Everything went great for six years until the king died. The incoming governors decided to issue a new daler that had less value than the previous issue. People wanting to cash in on their increase in value went to the bank to withdraw their dalers. When the customer withdrawals exceeded the amount on deposit the bank decided to lend more money out to cover the shortcoming. Eventually, the wheels stopped spinning and Palmstruch is arrested for fraud, sentenced to death and later pardoned. Palmstruch is later credited with the creation of the Wests first paper currency.

In 1694 the Bank of England was started as a private bank which provided banking support to the government. It was primarily founded to finance a war against France. It was the first government bank to make paper notes a permanent issuance. The issuance was denominated in pounds, which had been in use as a metal-based coin currency since the middle ages. The pound sterling is the world's oldest currency still in use. The pound sterling was originally backed by one pound of sterling silver (92.5% silver) it is now a fiat currency. In 1816 Great Britain adopted the Gold Standard which tokenized silver coins. A token is a coin that does not contain its value in precious metals.

The Dollar first enters the currency world during the War of Independence in 1775. The continental congress issued paper currency known as the "Continental", which was subsequently debased to the point that it had no value. By 1781 the Continental was so worthless it ceased being used as money. The term dollar, originating from the German Thaler, had been in use since colonial times and referred to eight-real (a Spanish coin). In 1792, U.S. Congress instituted the Dollar as the country's standard unit of currency and affixed its value to gold and silver. Lack of control over its creation debased the value, states were printing their own notes and coinage was still widely used as currency. This period is referred to as the bi-metallic period, instability in the supply of both metals played havoc on their values and by association the value of the dollar. During the civil war, Congress passed the

Legal Tender Act of 1862, taking the dollar off the bi-metallic standard and guaranteeing it only by the full faith and credit of the United States. Hyperinflation ensued as the Government printed an inordinate amount of paper notes. By 1879 the U.S. had returned to the gold standard and continued the practice until 1933. President Franklin D. Roosevelt made it illegal for U.S. citizens to own gold (besides jewelry) and stated that gold could only be used for international trade. This resulted in a buildup of gold in Fort Knox. By the 1970's the amassed gold started dwindling due to international trade and President Nixon announced that international countries could no longer exchange dollars for gold. This was the end of the gold standard and made the dollar a fiat currency, which is only backed by the full faith and credit of the United States.

The Federal Reserve System

Only when people have built up faith and confidence in a monetary medium is it possible for the authorities to take advantage of that faith.

– Glyn Davies

During the revolutionary period Alexander Hamilton, the Secretary of Treasury at the time called for a central authority to handle matters of the fledgling country's currency. As a result of his actions, the First Bank of the United States was chartered in 1791. The bank was privately owned but it was used as a tool by the government. After 20 years its charter expired, and the U.S. was without a central bank the economy suffered unusual inflation. There were several more attempts to institute a central bank with many failures. A financial crisis in 1907 was prevented by a private conglomerate of banks headed by J.P. Morgan who set themselves up as lenders of last resort. The Federal Reserve System was created by the Federal Reserve Act of 1913. The Federal Reserve Bank was instituted as the lender of last resort who would serve to protect banks by providing liquidity during periods of financial crisis.

The Federal Reserve System is mandated by Congress to perform five general functions to promote the effectiveness of the U.S. economy. It conducts the nations monetary policy to ensure maximum employment, stable prices, and moderate interest rates. It is charged with endorsing the stability of the financial system. It regulates private financial institutions to promote safety and soundness of the financial system. It ensures payment and settlement system safety and efficiency. Finally, it promotes consumer protection and community development. The Federal Reserve System is a quasi-government organization with many features of a privately held organization. It was set up to decentralize authority from one central bank into a system of national banks with a board of governors.

Monetary policy is the actions of the central authority, for any given currency, with the intent to control the rate of growth and supply of the money. As we learned earlier supply and demand affect value, so to control the supply of currency is to control the value. The Federal Reserve controls the value of the dollar by issuing bonds, manipulating the prime interest rate, buying and selling government bonds, and by changing the amount banks are required to keep in their vaults which are called the bank reserves. The institution of monetary policy by the Federal Reserve and the dollar not being tied to anything of value is a very distressing sign.

There are currently close to 14 Trillion U.S. Dollars in circulation. If that doesn't scare you consider the Debt to Gross Domestic Product ratio for the U.S. is 104%, meaning that the country could not pay off what it owes with what it produces. The World Bank calls anything over 77% a "Tipping Point". Runaway monetary policy and gross unchecked government spending are debasing the dollar in an incredible manner. If you are still not convinced, consider this; does it feel to you that your Dollars don't go as far as they used to. Do you ever think to yourself "How did my parents afford to live making less money than I do?" This is the value of your dollars going down through inflation. The Dollar is weakening, and it is only a matter of time before its value disappears. The dollar will go by the way of the Chinese failed experiments in paper currency.

Problems with Paper

Money often costs too much.
–Ralph Waldo Emerson

One thing is obvious, fiat currencies have many problems. This is important to note as it plays a role in what happens next. All fiat currencies will eventually burn out. The cycle of overprinting money, exorbitant government spending, unreal trade deficits, and the ticking time bomb that is the national debt will eventually bring down this house of cards. The Federal Reserve is doing what they can to keep the value of the Dollar in an appropriate range, but inflation and the overabundant supply of paper will eventually topple the almighty dollar. The current system, the dependence on fiat currencies is unsustainable. Problem number 1 is inflation and devaluation.

Another problem with fiat currencies is that they are restricted geographically. What I mean is this, if I go to China, I cannot use my dollars, they are useless there, I must convert my currency to their currency. Problem 2, paper money is locally based, meaning that it can only be spent where it originates.

Trying to send money to someone raises another problem of paper currency. For example; Say that I am going to send my family some money in another country. I would go to my bank, get the money set up to be sent, this involves a fee, the money is sent via wire transfer add another fee, the facilitating company charges another fee, my family's bank receives the money and charges a fee to retrieve it. If the amount is above a certain threshold then the IRS is notified and will want to talk to you about yet another fee (Taxes). There is no anonymity in paper currency, your bank knows you are sending money, the wire company knows your name, the other bank knows you, and sometimes the IRS can get involved and they all want to take a piece for themselves. Problem 3, no privacy in paper currency.

As we discussed, the banking industry has been around for a while. The banks charge fees for the safeguarding of people's money. They also have other instruments they use to create revenue, but we will focus on safeguarding money. Banking collapses in the past aside, they do a pretty good job of it. What must be understood is that they control people's money. This is an outlandish example but hear me out, the bank can decide to close their doors forever and keep all the money they hold for their customers. Like I said outlandish, or is it, here is an exercise go to google and type in "Bank closed my account" or "Bank Failures" and look at the results. The truth is that they cannot keep your money if the bank is Federally Insured (FDIC), but even then, it could take months to recover what you lost. Problem 4, banks, not you, safeguard your money.

Close to $16 Billion was stolen in 2017 alone through fraud and identity theft. Another drawback of paper currency is that if you carry a lot of it, you may as well paint a target on your back. Theft is a major problem in the world and paper currency is very susceptible to being stolen. Problem 5, any money you own can be stolen through robbery or through identity theft.

Digital Cash

With e-currency based on cryptographic proof,
without the need to trust a third-party middleman,
money can be secure and transactions effortless.

– Satoshi Nakamoto

In 2008, the markets were disastrous, there seemed to be a new company going under every other day. Big companies and financial institutions took huge gambles on some securities that were based on very bad mortgage loans. When these loans started to default it made the securities, which were bundling them up by the thousands, insolvent and those companies got left holding the bag and could not unload them. The government, against popular opinion, decided that they could not allow some of these large companies to become insolvent and stepped in to bail them out. That's all in the past but what it does is set the scene for how and why Bitcoin was created.

In 2008, Satoshi Nakamoto, a shadowy character whose real identity is unknown, released the technology that will change the system and the world. Bitcoin came to be on the backdrop of financial disaster, and rampant central banks enforcing reckless monetary policies. We will be discussing Bitcoin in more detail later, but for now here is a brief introduction. Bitcoin solves many problems of traditional fiat currency or "paper money", one being decentralizing the authority or control of the currency. By using the blockchain technology (more on this later) Bitcoin can spread the control of the currency throughout the entire blockchain, this means that there is not one individual or institution who can control the supply of money in the system or make any decisions which will affect the currency in any way. Essentially once the code is online the cryptocurrency cannot be changed. As we will discuss later, this is both an advantage and a disadvantage.

Another advantage that Bitcoin introduced was the fact that it exists online, meaning it is a digital currency. There are no physical Bitcoin tokens, it is all on computer code which is cryptographically encrypted for security. It is truly a global currency. There are no borders, with Bitcoin I can buy a product in China while living in the United States.

Technology Changes Industry and Markets

The advance of technology is based on making it fit in so that you don't really even notice it, so it's part of everyday life.

– Bill Gates

So how does cryptocurrency change anything, isn't it just another market fad? Well, no, the reason this is going to change everything is because it is the next progression in the evolution of the markets. To see why this is we must look at other industries. Let's look at the medical industry, for example, 150 years ago a doctor could only diagnose a patient based on symptoms. A person suffering from something would go to the doctor and describe what was wrong and based on those symptoms the doctor would make an educated guess. Based on his knowledge from medical school the doctor would treat the patient for what he thought was wrong. Now, because of technological advancements, a doctor has many tools he can use to aide him in identifying his patient's ailments. A doctor can look inside the body with an MRI or an X-Ray, they can identify blood clots inside the brain with a Cat Scan, they can test nerves with a TIMS machine. These technologies have made doctors more accurate with their diagnosis and as a result people are living longer. Research is being conducted now on Nanotechnology and its applications in the field of medicine. This will again revolutionize the medical industry. Technology has changed and continues to change the medical industry.

We can look at the retail industry. Amazon has put many brick-and-mortar retail companies out of business and many others are struggling to stay afloat (think Best Buy). Again, a technological advancement, the online shopping platform, has changed an entire industry. The television industry is amid a major change as well. Companies like Netflix, Sling TV, YouTube, Amazon Prime, and Hulu are changing the way television is consumed. Many entertainment companies are seeking more a-la-carte delivery systems, either by partnering with Netflix and the like or by creating their own online channels (see HBO Go, ESPN and Disney are also creating new online channels). Technological advances are changing these and many more industries.

Technology Creates Industry and Markets

Every once in a while, a new technology, an old problem,
and a big idea turn into an innovation.

– Dean Kamen

Technological advances can also create new industries. For example, scientific research into robotics has created an entirely new industry, that being the Unmanned Aerial Vehicle segment. UAV's are not just for hobbyists or kids anymore, the U.S. Government is investing billions into UAV technology. The military uses drones for reconnaissance, troop protection, mission support, and target delivery. Private and public companies contract out to the U.S. military for products and services. The Department of Agriculture uses drones to conduct aerial surveys of farmland. The Census Bureau uses drones to conduct aerial surveys of major metropolitan areas. Various government and state law enforcement agencies use drones for mission support and reconnaissance. Although new the global UAV market value had reached $70 Billion by 2017.

Another instance is the internet, we have all heard of the dot-com boom. The internet began as a military project with the goal of improving communication during wartime. When the technology was introduced to the public innovators saw an opportunity and the internet introduced the world to the digital age. The internet created a new market and continues to introduce new avenues and new markets to the world. At last check Amazon, Google, and Apple are all competing to be the first trillion-dollar company, all three are tech companies two of them are internet companies.

Buyers Beware

"On Wall Street, financial crisis destroys jobs.
Here in Washington, it creates them. The rest is just details."

– Timothy Noah

The last time the financial world saw such extreme gains as we are seeing in the cryptocurrency market was the internet boom. From 1995 until the year 2000 the Nasdaq (the technology index) rose from under 1,000 all the way to 5,000. That is an incredible climb in 5 years, to put that into perspective the Nasdaq today sits at 7,239. In the 18 years since the end of the dot-com bubble, it has only risen another 2,239 points. The commercialization of the internet led to the greatest expansion of capital growth the country had ever seen. From 1995 until 2000 the market was fed by overzealous investors, and venture capitalists looking to find the next big score. Anything with a ".com" at the end was pumped up by cheap money and over speculation all the while completely ignoring fundamentals. Companies which had yet to turn a profit or have a finished product went to market with initial public offerings and saw their stock prices more than triple in one day. It all came to a head early in the year 2000, when some of the bigger investors in the market sold their large shares causing panic selling which resulted in the market losing 10% of its value. The money dried up for cash-strapped dot-com companies and a great majority crumbled, going from a market capitalization in the hundreds of millions to worthless in a matter of months.

It wasn't all bad news though, out of the ashes rose some of the biggest companies we know of today. Companies like Amazon and Google who are now competing to break the trillion-dollar capitalization mark. Imagine if you were able to pick from the thousands of companies in the market to find and invest in the good ones like Amazon and Google.

The internet was a bubble, everyone knows it now as the dot-com bubble. There were many companies who saw a huge influx of investors just by adding ".com" to their name. The point is that when there is a bubble that's as big as the internet and cryptocurrencies (which I believe will be a bigger market than the internet) it attracts scumbags. During the internet bubble, there was a lot of companies that were started just to make money for their founders. They had no purpose, no business structure, and no way of ever becoming successful. Yet investors pumped them up and their stock prices grew thereby making their founders rich. Eventually, the market gets wise to them and they will ultimately fail. The same thing will happen in the cryptocurrency market. Whenever there is money to be made there will be scummy people who will try to scam folks to get rich.

There are many coins which are worthless, they serve no purpose, solve no problems, yet they will be bought up in the mania of the bubble. It will take time for the market to shake out all the bad apples. This is completely preventable, by doing your due diligence and research you can at least ensure that you will not be scammed. Unfortunately, there is no way to guarantee winning, it is a market after all. It is important to learn how to do your research, and how to establish some criteria or a system to invest your money.

Summary

Large numbers of strangers can cooperate successfully by believing in common myths. Any large-scale human cooperation – whether a modern state, a medieval church, an ancient city or an archaic tribe – is rooted in common myths that exist only in people's collective imagination.

– Yuval Noah Harari

Currency is a myth, a myth the entire world believes in. We have been led to believe that a meaningless paper note with some signatures and figures on it represents something of value and a medium for exchange. Currency is a tool that is used for trade in markets. The belief that it has worth gives it the value it needs to work as a tool for trade. In the beginning, the value was proportional to what you traded for, in the barter system. When markets grew a new tool was needed to facilitate the growth and coins were introduced. As the world grew bigger and international trade became more common another evolution was needed to facilitate the growth, introduce precious metals. As international trade grew larger precious metals were limiting, currency evolved into paper notes backed by precious metals. With the industrial revolution and the introduction of the corporate age more money was needed than the system could accommodate, money evolved again into paper notes unpegged from precious metals, the modern fiat currency. The internet introduced humanity into the digital age, money is evolving again into digital currency secured by cryptographic cipher, cryptocurrency.

Traditionally the transition or evolution of currency is slow, it takes time for the public to become accustomed to new systems and ways of thinking. The transition to fiat currency took almost 200 years, and there are still many who think we should go back to precious metals backing currency more than 50 years after unpegging them. At the precipice of every human innovation, currency has had to evolve to solve the problems that stagnate growth. Throughout history we see the problems that limit fiat currency, we see fiat currencies rise and fall. History is deemed to repeat itself, the current system will eventually fall. Listed below are the most prominent problems with the current system of fiat currency.

Problems with paper money:

1. Inflation and devaluation
2. Locally based
3. No privacy
4. Banks, not you, safeguard your money
5. Theft

We talked about how technology and innovation can change industry and markets. We saw that technology and innovation can create new markets. These two points are important because this is what is currently happening in the cryptocurrency sphere. Bitcoin introduced an innovation to the currency industry, the technology behind Bitcoin is changing and evolving the currency industry. Meanwhile, it is also creating a new market. The cryptocurrency market is very different than the stock market. When you buy a share of a company in the stock market, you own a portion of that company. This is not always the case when you buy a cryptocurrency. It is important to know what you are buying and what it gets you.

Cryptocurrency is here to stay, for the very reasons I highlighted here. It is not a fad, it is the next evolution in currency. Fiat currencies will eventually break and lose all value because they hold no true value, they are backed by governments and economies. What happens when those economies decide to go digital. Cryptocurrencies that solve real-world problems will flourish and lead all humanity into the future.

CHAPTER 3

DEVELOPING A SYSTEM

Formal education will make you a living;
self-education will make you a fortune.

– Jim Rohn

Trying to invest in the markets without a system is the equivalent of sprinting across a busy intersection blindfolded during rush hour trying not to get hit by a car. You are going to get clipped, at least once, and that makes for a bad day. In the markets, whether it be the stock market or the cryptocurrency market there is always a winner and a loser. Say an investor holds a big position in a stock and wants to start unloading it based on some negative news he knows about, you have not heard the news and buy his position up, the stock then loses value as the news hits the market. The investor knew the news was coming out, he took his gains and dumped the stock and you were left holding the bag.

The same thing can happen in the crypto market. Like I mentioned before there are many coins that are worthless, yet these coins can be pumped up for profits. Investors will buy up the coins then go on a campaign to increase the price per token, once they get it to a certain threshold they proceed to dump the tokens on unsuspecting investors. They take their gains and move on to the next coin. This is one example of some scummy behavior, which is frowned upon in the general market. The general market wants to get rid of this kind of ridiculous behavior because it detracts from what we all want, mass adoption, then we all make money. Fortunately for us, this situation is easy to spot but there are other tactics used to scam people. The best way to combat these unscrupulous tactics is to have a good system for determining what and how to invest your money.

Research for the Win!

Opportunity is missed by most people
because it is dressed in overalls and looks like work.

– Thomas Edison

Your due diligence begins with your research. The thing to remember when conducting your research is to know the sources. Consider who you are reading information from, do they stand to profit from you investing in a certain cryptocurrency. There are people in the market that make money through commissions, referral fees, or marketing fees for getting people to buy a certain coin. There is a practice called bounty hunting. Bounty hunters are rewarded with coins in exchange for marketing certain cryptocurrencies. Using a bounty hunter campaign gives developers the power of social marketing. There are also people who will artificially "pump" a coin to increase the value because they own it and want to sell it for higher. This is called a "pump and dump" and is usually a red flag that the coin is no good (shitcoin).

You make your money in cryptocurrency when you buy the coins, not when you sell them. You want to ensure you are buying at a good discounted value. To do this you must know what you are looking for in a good coin. You must establish some criteria of what makes a good coin for investment. Here is a solid foundation to start with, with this you can build your own system to qualify your investments.

- **Go to the source:** Go to the developer's website. If they have a good website, it will be full of information about their product and their plans. If they don't have a good website, that's a red flag.

- **Read the whitepaper:** The whitepaper goes into detail about their product, how the tokens will be used, what problems they solve, their timeline for execution, and much more useful information. The whitepapers can get technical at times so try to skim the technical stuff and get to the good information.

- **Meet the developers:** Reputable developers will provide information about themselves and their backgrounds. Don't be afraid to google them, or review their social media profiles, LinkedIn is a very useful social media tool in this category. Most reputable developers provide their social media links in their bios on the website.

- **Get a second opinion:** Find out what other people are saying about the token you are research-ing. This is where it is important to understand where your information is coming from. Some good websites to visit are cryptocompare.com and coinmarketcap.com.

This is all well and good, but you will be doing a lot of meaningless reading unless you know what to look for. So here is a foundation to start qualifying candidates:

- **Does it solve a problem of fiat currency:** Fiat currency has many problems, as we have discussed.

A good benchmark for a coin's future worth is if it solves one or more of these problems.

- **Does it solve a Bitcoin problem:** Bitcoin solved some of the problems with fiat currency, but it does not solve them all and it also introduced new problems. Many new currencies have been introduced that were built off the Bitcoin platform to solve some of the Bitcoin problems.

- **Is there a limited supply:** The token you are looking at should have a limited supply of coins with no way of artificially creating more. There will only ever be 21 million Bitcoin, it has a hard cap there. This is a limited supply, there can never be any more than 21 million Bitcoin. The token you are evaluating should have a limited supply. Scarcity creates value.

- **Are you investing in a platform or a currency:** Many developers have excellent ideas, you would have never thought there could be so much creativity in the world. The problem is that we are looking for a currency, not an idea to revolutionize the shipping industry or anything else. Developers raise money for their ideas by offering coins, their hope is that the coins will gain value for their buyers in the open market. In other words, you are not getting shares, or a part of the company, or even profit sharing by buying their coins. This is not the stock market. Do not fall in love with their ideas. I made this mistake, I fell in love with an idea and invested my money in a coin that is not a currency.

Note: Some of these coins are good for trading and can sometimes gain decent value in the market.

- **Is it useful:** The search for the cryptocurrency that will replace the current system of currencies is still on. The one currency that will replace all world currencies and become the global currency has not been found, yet. If a cryptocurrency solves all the problems of paper money, and all the problems Bitcoin introduced, plus it has a limited supply then this currency will be set to become the global currency. Hopefully you and I both will be holding it when it does.

This is a brief overview of how to conduct research and where to find the information you would need. It, at least, lays the groundwork for you to establish some standards to develop a system. It is imperative you use your own judgment when qualifying investment candidates. If something smells fishy, or if it sounds too good to be true then it probably isn't true. The important thing is to use the biggest asset you have, your brain. Now that we have a research plan we can start working on an investment plan.

Creating an Investment Plan

You try to be greedy when others are fearful.
And you try to be fearful when others are greedy.
— Warren Buffett

Developing an investment strategy is difficult but the benefits outweigh the hard work you put in by a mile. Confidence comes from having a plan, the confidence you will enjoy from having a system will ensure that you will recover quickly from any misstep or mistake because you can always fall back on your plan. You will understand that sticking to the plan and staying the course is the best path to success. Cryptocurrency is a new market segment, it is different than the stock market, it reacts differently to news, the volatility is different, price action is different, and as of now, there is no government regulation of this market. That being the case there is currently no real investment plans to follow. I can tell you what I am doing, and I have some other ideas of how to grow your money.

Buy and Hodl - As mentioned in Chapter 1, I believe this is the beginning of a long run in the crypto market. My plan is the traditional buy and hodl plan (**h**old **o**n for **d**ear **l**ife, no I didn't misspell it, it's a common term used in crypto) that is preached by most of the financial wizards of the stock market. Obviously, this would involve finding and holding the right cryptocurrency. To do this I do my research, as illustrated above. I read the whitepapers, I study the coin and its application, I see if the coin solves any problems of fiat currency, I see if the coin solves any problems of Bitcoin or Ethereum, I review the team, I use my good judgment. Once I run a coin through my prequalification gambit I then purchase the coin and hold for the long term. Whenever the markets go down I don't panic, in fact, I celebrate because it means I can buy more at a discount. I follow the wise words of Warren Buffet; I am greedy and buy when others are fearful and are panic selling.

This doesn't mean I won't try other investment strategies, only that most of my money will be going to my plan. If I have extra money and I am willing to gamble a little I will try some of these other strategies.

Note: I have tried some other strategies, granted with very little money, for research for this book and the other books I have in mind for the future. I don't want my readers to think that I am on a soapbox or trying to tell people what to do and not doing it myself.

Dividend Investing – Dividend investing is quite popular in the stock market. Essentially an investor buys stock in blue chip companies who reward their shareholders with dividends from their earnings. Dividend investing is possible in the cryptocurrency market as well. Currencies like Neo are spearheading this type of investment. More on Neo later, just know that if you own Neo tokens and have them in your Neon wallet they will reward you with Gas tokens. Gas is the, well the gas in the Neo blockchain, and it is a crypto token that is traded in most major exchanges. There are other cryptocurrencies doing this same kind of reward (dividend) system. This is a good way to let your money work for you. Just buy the Neo let it sit in your wallet and get paid Gas for owning it.

Miners – In the Bitcoin and Ethereum blockchain miners validate transactions and create blocks that go on the chain. For this activity, miners get rewarded with coins. The cryptocurrency market is here to stay and as such miners will be an integral part of the system for some time to come. Knowing this it would seem a good idea to start investing in them. There are several ways to do this, more to come in the next book when we will dive in deeper into this sector.

- **Initial Coin Offerings (ICO):** ICO's are a way for token companies to raise funds to set their platform off. ICO's for miners are becoming more popular, some have even begun to offer partial ownership or stakes in their business as an incentive to invest.

- **Buying Miners Coins in an exchange:** After their ICO, some of the miners opt to list their coins on exchanges to be traded like other coins, this allows coins to gain value. Of course, they could also lose value in the open market. Once the ICO is complete they cannot revisit the ICO structure again to raise capital, and buyers cannot buy any more coins unless they are in an exchange.

- **Joining a Cloud Miner group:** Cloud mining consists of renting out processing power from established mining companies. These companies have already established platforms, have the equipment, and the expertise in mining cryptocurrency. The terms usually come in units of hash rates, Mega hashes and Giga hashes have different pricing terms. You get paid in the crypto of your choice, according to how much processing power you lease from them.

- **Setting up a mining rig** – Setting up a mining rig can be difficult and costly. If you don't know what you are doing it could be a disaster. Mining rigs usually cost between $3,000 and $5,000 for a small rig which you can set up in your garage. A small rig, between 6 and 8 GPU's (Graphics Processors) can net about $3,000 per year. Depending on the current value of the crypto you are mining, it could be more if it goes up or less if it goes down. The net profits could also be affected by the cost of electricity for cooling your rig, for example, if you live in a hot environment it will cost more to cool the rig down. Once you have set up your rig you would join a mining pool to collect your currency. This can be a profitable venture if you know what you are doing.

Note: when calculating your expense remember to include the cost of electricity, the mining pool fees, as well as your wallet transfer fees.

- **Invest in mining companies on stock exchanges:** Yes, there are some mining companies who have chosen to go public to attract capital. This is a new trend and it is gaining momentum. At this point they are rare and hard to find, you will not find them on the NASDAQ. Some can be found on the Toronto Stock Exchange TSX, more on these later.

Investing in ICO: Initial Coin Offerings can provide a good avenue to make a decent chunk of money. If you do your homework and research the company, and you believe in their platform an ICO offers a path for you to get in on the ground floor. On the other hand, ICO's can also provide a quick payday. When the new coin is out of the ICO stage it will be listed on an exchange, their prices are usually fractions of a penny, so their prices swing wildly and can sometimes gain 100 to 200 percent or more in a day. If you buy a coin during an ICO, at a stable price and most of the time at a discount or with a bonus, then hold it until it is listed on an exchange, you can sell it once it gains value on the open market for a quick profit. You will want to ensure that the developers plan on listing the coins in an exchange. Not all coins are listed, and some developers do not plan on listing their coins. Just as any other investment this strategy does come with some risk, do your own due diligence and research. It is also imperative to understand how ICO's work and where you stand as a public investor. The first to get in are venture capitalists, then come institutional investors, and finally the investment is opened to the public. If you understand where you stand and how it works, and you are fine with it there is money to be made from this strategy.

Trading Cryptocurrency: Trading in the cryptocurrency market can be very profitable. The crypto market has extreme volatility at times and the wild price swings provide an excellent opportunity to make some quick money. Trading stocks in the stock exchange is difficult and that is a regulated exchange which has been established for many years. The cryptocurrency market is very new, and it is not regulated. Trading in the crypto market can be very dangerous, but if you have a high tolerance for risk then it can pay off. Do not trade until you have done your homework and understand how to do it, it is not the same as the stock exchange.

Obviously, this is a very short introduction to investing in cryptocurrency, we will dive deeper into most of these topics in later chapters and later books.

When we do, I will give you more detailed information about developers, companies, and processes. This a way to jump-start your research and get you thinking about how to profit from this market.

The choice is yours, how you chose to invest in this new market is trivial. The important thing is to BE in this market. There is too much money to be made to be sitting on the sidelines watching everyone else get wealthy. Get active, get learning, and get investing. If I can do it, you can do it. It is all a matter of getting active, this book is a good first step for learning, I just don't want you to stop here.

CHAPTER 4

WHAT NEWS?

Fear tends to manifest itself much more quickly than greed,
so volatile markets tend to be on the downside. In up markets,
volatility tends to gradually decline.

– Philip Roth

So now we know how to create a system for investing in cryptocurrency, but if you are feeding that system bad news from untrustworthy sources then the system will not produce good results. In the stock market, by the time you can get access to the news and information it is usually already too late, the market has already reacted to it and you have missed the opportunity. There is a saying in the investment world "buy the rumors and sell the news". It is a different situation in the cryptocurrency markets. The actionable news you will be getting will, for the most part, come from the source, the developers, meaning that you will be able to act in the market when you get the information. This will not always be the case, as the market matures actionable information will slow down. This is the perfect time to get into the market. Next, we will look at some news and information resources for conducting your pre-buying research, there will also be some sources where you can hear rumors, share and hear ideas, get involved in the crypto community, and hopefully get some actionable information to make some money.

Before we begin we must lay some ground rules, these are more like common sense guidelines. As this is a very new market, not everything you hear may be appropriate to try and you should use some restraint in some cases. Use your common sense if something smells fishy, or sounds too good to be true, then you should slow down and think hard before taking any sort of action. Be wary of people trying to pump a certain token's price up, this action called "pump and dump" is very common in some of these sources. Do not ever give away your coins to anyone, there are some people who will post giveaways; something to the tune of "send me your coins and you will get double back". If you fall for that one, email me I have some beachfront property in Arizona I'd like to talk to you about. I say that, but I fell for one, it looked legit but turned out to be a scam. Fortunately, I only lost about $10 worth of coins. Do not ever sign up for a giveaway by posting your private key on a social site. Your private keep should be closely guarded and not for the public, all your funds will disappear.

Another practice I have started using is to paper trade some of the ideas I hear. I will make a log entry into my investment or trade book as if I am putting money into the token based on the buy and sell signals. Once the paper trade is completed I will know if I can trust the individual giving the signals. When doing this make sure to give them more than one chance, a buy and sell signal is not always accurate, they may not always be right. If you give them more than one chance you will quickly determine if they are a trusted source or a pump and dump chump.

Once you have been in the community for a while you will naturally start learning who to trust for information, buy and sell signals, and for general knowledge. This is a very new space and there are not many trusted and professional services for information, this is an opportunity for some as it could provide an avenue into this market without risking too much capital, more on that later.

Resources for Learning

Live as if you were to die tomorrow.
Learn as if you were to live forever.

– Mahatma Gandhi

The way I learned and continue to learn is through reading as much information as I could consume daily. I read articles or guides online and if I didn't understand something or a topic sounded interesting I would Google it and read some more. That said, here are some references for you.

Coindesk – Coindesk is a wealth of information for beginners in the crypto markets and for blockchain enthusiasts. If you go to Blockchain 101 in the main menu you will find some good introductions into the blockchain, Bitcoin, and Ethereum. Coindesk is a resource for learning and information as well. (www.coindesk.com)

Coinbase – Coinbase is not just an exchange where you can buy Bitcoin and Ethereum, it is also an excellent place to start learning about cryptocurrency. On the Coinbase website in the footer menu find the Blog hyperlink. In the blog section, there is a wealth of knowledge about getting started in the crypto market. (www.coinbase.com)

Medium – Medium is a website that collects information, mostly in the form of articles, written and submitted by regular people some who are experts, some are market participants, and some who are just enthusiasts. These articles are written and displayed based on your interests. There are many articles written every day about cryptocurrency, there are some good writers on there that you can learn from. Many developers post articles on Medium with the goal of explaining their projects and platforms. This is a great avenue to learn about some of the latest advancements in the market directly from the source. When you sign up for Medium, you can choose topics that interest you, from there you will get only articles on topics that you are interested in. (www.medium.com)

Resources for Information

If people in the media cannot decide whether they are in the business of reporting news or manufacturing propaganda, it is all the more important that the public understand that difference and choose their news sources accordingly.

– Thomas Sowell

Crypto Currency News – Crypto Currency News is a lot like Coindesk in that it provides good articles and good information. There is much more opinion-based news on this site compared to Coindesk. There is also price analysis for different coins. I would start my research on Coindesk and move to this site for further details. This site is excellent for getting investment ideas and good for price analysis. (cryptocurrencynews.com)

Note: I began my learning on the cryptocurrency news mobile application on my android phone. The app draws news articles from different reputable news sources and pools them together, so you can view them on your phone. It is a great application to get information on the go.

Coin Telegraph – Coin Telegraph is another news website much the same as Coindesk and Crypto Currency News, with a few tweaks. This site has a cool feature in which you can pick the news category you want to read about. There are categories to get news for Bitcoin, Ethereum, alternative coins, scam information, government regulation, and more. This is a nice feature if you know exactly what you are looking for. (cointelegraph.com)

CCN – CCN, not to be confused with CNN, is another news website. I have not used CCN much before, so I cannot tell you much here. They have an ICO calendar that looks interesting, and they are looking for full-time journalists and editors, a possibility to make money without investing, or maybe you can just do their James Earl Jones voice-over "This is CCN". (www.ccn.com)

Coin Market Cap – Coin Market Cap is where you go to get price and charting services for the crypto markets. There is no news here, this is only to find technical price information along with information about which exchanges support the coin you are researching. This should be your first stop when you find an investment, find out where it is trading, how the price is moving, and how it compares to other cryptocurrencies. (coinmarketcap.com)

My advice for news sources is obviously just a recommendation. It is up to each of you to determine what good news sources are. From those good sources which ones provide the most reliable information.

Community Resources

The cryptocurrency community hasn't decided whether they want to be anarchist rebels or to replace the establishment.

– Adi Shamir

Cryptocurrency community resources provide useful and actionable information. At times this information will come in the form of rumors. Sometimes it will be directly from the developers and their plans.

63

It is important to be in these communities to pick up on the trends of the market, where the market is going, and if there is anything new that might take off. Imagine if you could have had a direct line to Jeff Bezos when Amazon was first starting out. Imagine if you could ask him direct questions about the company. Imagine if he would have shared the company's plan or the Amazon roadmap on a social website. This is what these community resources provide; most developers promote their projects, platforms, and tokens on these websites and you can be in the loop for free. Just as in any other situation involving investments, use caution and common sense when acting upon information learned on these sites.

Telegram - Telegram is an instant messaging social platform known for its security. The platform quickly syncs the activity between your mobile phone and the desktop sites. It is a preferred social media platform for the cryptocurrency community. Many groups have been started for crypto enthusiasts which cover information about the markets, technical price analysis, buy and sell signals, reviews of upcoming ICO's, and even bounty and airdrop announcements to get free coins.

Some developers create groups for their tokens on Telegram to begin marketing, or to communicate with their followers. This is an excellent source of useful and actionable information that comes straight from the source.

When you first create your account on Telegram, go to the search bar and look for Crypto Communities and Crypto Groups. Join these two channels as they have lists of all the cryptocurrency related groups and update it often as more are created. When you find a cryptocurrency, you may be interested in, look for them on Telegram, as they may have a channel where you can find more information. (web.telegram.org)

Crypto Chasers Confidential - Crypto Chasers Confidential is a team of software engineers and investors that provide high quality fundamental analysis reports for altcoins along with market updates. I first came across CCC on Telegram, they have a channel there where they distribute their analysis. They also have a premium service, CCC VIP is still free but they only allow a certain amount of people to join. (crypto-chasers.net)

Twitter - Twitter is another social media platform; crypto enthusiasts are not as active on Twitter as they are on Telegram but if you follow the right people you can find some useful information. (www.twitter.com)

Discord - Discord is a free voice and chat application for gamers. Although it is mostly used by gamers there are crypto enthusiast groups on Discord. One such group is Cosmic Trading, they have some good information available for anyone from beginner to expert. (discordapp.com)

Hacker Noon - Hacker Noon is allegedly a hacker website, their slogan is "how hackers start their afternoons". It is a very good website with some great tech content. Many of the articles originated on Hacker Noon are featured on Medium. There are great articles on the blockchain, cryptocurrency, venture capital, and artificial intelligence. Some of the information is very technical but they have a section called WTF. We all know what that stands for but, in this section, there are good articles explaining a lot of the things we may not understand. Those articles are meant to provide a better overall understanding of the technology landscape. (www.hackernoon.com)

All the resources listed here are absolutely free, there are some other providers that do charge for services. Most of these service providers teach you the basics about the market, then set you up on their trading or investment strategy. There are also mentorship programs that charge service fees. These kind of service providers, although sometimes worth the money, are not my preferred method of learning. I prefer to make my own strategies, that is not to say they have no value, they could provide some people with the means they need to make a decent return.

News and information moves markets, it happens in the stock market and it happens in the cryptocurrency market. Early access to the information in the crypto market can provide a definitive edge to a trader and a long-term investor. Early access can give an investor a chance to buy their investment at a low price, or an opportunity to buy more on a dip in price. It would allow a trader to buy something on a dip and sell at the high for a quick return. The importance of accurate and early information and news cannot be understated. Now that we have a good foundation for our investing system supported by some accurate news we can move on to learn all about cryptocurrency.

CHAPTER 5

THE BLOCKCHAIN

*Blockchain is the tech. Bitcoin is merely the first
mainstream manifestation of its potential.*

–Marc Kenigsberg

If databases were regular humans like you and me,
then the blockchain would be Superman. Sorry,
my son is into superheroes so it's easy for me to make
those kinds of analogies. Blockchain was the technological advancement that Nakamoto introduced, not
Bitcoin. Cryptocurrency is just one application or use
of the blockchain. That said, the blockchain was not
a new discovery. In truth, it is a melding and repur-
posing of three different older technologies. Those
technologies being the internet, cryptography, and
governing protocol. The blockchain is a peer to peer
network (P2P) of transaction validation nodes secured
by cryptographic keys. The nodes are then rewarded
for validating the transactions, thereby adding another
layer of protection. Sounds fancy and more than a

little technical, I know. Trust me, if you get into it, the blockchain can get very difficult, so I will try to make it as simple as possible.

Let's take a real-world example to demonstrate the viability of the blockchain. Say, for example, you are buying a home. You put in a contract for the home you want to buy, the contract goes to the sellers who sign the contract accepting the terms. The contract must be validated by a third party, usually a title company. The title company has many lawyers who run through the contract and ensure everything is accurate. The title company ensures the sellers conveying the property truly own the property, there are no liens on the property, and run the transaction through a long checklist of items to ensure the property can be sold. Once complete they issue a clear title which signals that the property can be legally sold. Once a clear title is given the contract goes to the mortgage broker who qualifies the buyers through underwriting. The underwriters run through a gambit of qualifying requirements and finally produce a clear to close, meaning that the funds are available to complete the transaction. Once the clear to close is given then the title company meets with the buyers and sellers to convey title (ownership) to the buyers during the closing.

That is a long and arduous process which usually takes around twenty to thirty days of intense stress both for the buyers and the sellers. Now imagine if we ran that same transaction through the blockchain. The buyers submit a request to buy the property, in this request would be the buyers cryptographic key which holds the information needed for the transaction, funds, address, sellers consent to the contract, their agreement (the contract), and anything else that would be needed. The request is broadcast to a P2P network consisting of computers, known as nodes. The network of nodes would then validate the transaction, doing everything the title and mortgage companies did. The transaction, now validated, gets packaged with other transactions to become one block in a long chain of blocks. Once the validated transaction is on the blockchain it becomes a legally enforceable contract because of the immutability of the blockchain. This means that once something hits the blockchain it can never be changed. The transaction now becomes a legal contract ready for execution. The buyers now own the home.

This is an example of the power of the blockchain. This technology has use cases in anything that involves contracts or anything that uses a database. The blockchain is just a large, shared, cryptographically secured database. The distributed ledger is the most important innovation in blockchain technology. Anyone can see the transactions on the blockchain, but no one can ever change them. The nodes get compensated for the validation process, this is known as a mining fee. This compensation for validation adds another layer of security. If the nodes were not rewarded for their work, they would not have a vested interest in the validation process. Compensating the miners gives them a vested interest in the validation process thereby making the entire network more secure.

The transaction blocks are linked together in a chain going back to the first ever transaction. This means that if a hacker wanted to tamper with any single record he would have to be able to penetrate all the blocks in the chain, which is impossible even for a supercomputer. This makes the entire blockchain very secure. During the validation process, the network of nodes must come to a consensus or 51% approval before the transaction can be validated and processed. The way the nodes, or miners, validate the transactions is a complicated process that involves complicated algorithms, I will spare you the details. Suffice it to say that to be a miner you need access to a lot of processing power and cheap electricity. It takes a lot of electricity to keep the computers from overheating.

The Distributed Ledger

There is an opportunity to recreate the financial world as
we know it in the parallel universe that is the blockchain.
We are writing rules for this whole new universe.

– Patrick M. Byrne

If you have ever dealt with a database, you will know how frustrating it can be making changes from different nodes in the network. Regular databases are controlled by a central node on a network. The central node gives permissions to the external nodes to update the database, but no two nodes can update at the same time. Also, the external nodes do not communicate with each other, everything must go to the central node before every external node is updated. This can be frustrating as many of the different departments could potentially be working on old information because their nodes have not been updated by the central node.

The distributed ledger is a database that is independently held and updated by each individual node in a large network. Clear as mud, let me clarify. What this means is that the distributed ledger is a database that can be updated by any node in the network in real time. The database is no longer centralized, there is no central computer controlling the database and all other nodes. Every node on the network processes every transaction, they come to their own conclusions then vote on the conclusions to ensure a majority decision is reached. Once consensus is reached (51% majority) then the distributed ledger is updated, and all nodes maintain a copy of the ledger.

In our current system, we incur a cost of trust. The trustee's in our culture are notaries, bankers, the government, lawyers, etc. The architecture of the distributed ledger nullifies the cost of trust because the trust is distributed throughout the entire network. The entire network must reach a consensus before approving a transaction. A database must be maintained to function properly, the example above illustrates this. The distributed ledger represents a revolution in data, we concentrate less on maintaining the database and dedicate more time to interacting, using, and manipulating the information.

As we can see the blockchain provides for an easier transaction that is more secure, all while not involving a central point of authority or third-party approval. These facts open the blockchain up to endless possibilities. That is why people are so excited about this innovation.

Cryptocurrency is only the tip of the iceberg of what the blockchains can do. The list of industries the blockchain could benefit is endless. Imagine an airline booking system running on the efficiency and security of the blockchain. Logistics companies could benefit greatly with the ability to track supplies and shipping products on a distributed system. Different logistics companies could share the information contained in the blockchain because it is a distributed public ledger. The possibilities are endless, and the technology introduced by the blockchain is very exciting.

The blockchain provides the security, and efficiency for cryptocurrency to be viable for transactions. The fact that it is decentralized solves some of the problems of fiat currency mentioned earlier. The distributed quality of the transaction process removes unwanted third parties from our transactions, secures them, ensures transparency, and decentralizes them. Cryptocurrency backed by the blockchain has all the attributes needed to make it a suitable replacement for fiat currency.

CHAPTER 6

INTRODUCTION TO CRYPTOCURRENCY

A community is defined by the cooperation of its participants, and efficient cooperation requires a medium of exchange (money) and a way to enforce contracts.

– Wei Dai

Wei Dai, is a computer engineer and developer of the Crypto++ library. He worked for Microsoft where he developed several patents for the company. He is a big proponent of using cryptography in different aspects of culture and life to achieve social and political change. In 1998, Dai published b-money, distributed electronic cash system. In the paper Dai outlines the foundation of what modern cryptocurrencies rely upon. A network to facilitate the exchange of cash units to pay each other and enforce contracts without the need of third party involvement all secured by cryptographic hash. He based this idea on the concept of crypto-anarchy, not the type of anarchy that causes death and destruction, but the type of anarchy where the government is no longer needed. He proposed that to make the government permanently unnecessary, he needed a medium of exchange and a way to enforce contracts. The b-money protocol introduced:

- A specified amount of computational work to create monetary units (Proof of Work)

- The work to be verified by the community who then update a collective ledger (The Blockchain)

- Exchange of money is regulated by collective bookkeeping and authenticated by cryptographic hashes (Decentralized Transactions)

- The use of digital signatures on the transactions broadcast to the network to enforce contracts (Public and private keys)

This paper was published ten years before Bitcoin was introduced to the world. Satoshi Nakamoto credited Wei Dai and b-money in his whitepaper introducing Bitcoin. The list above is exactly what cryptocurrency is based on. Computational work to create money is mining, proof of work is used to create new Bitcoin along with many other cryptocurrencies. The collective ledger and collective bookkeeping are handled by the blockchain and the nodes or miners servicing the blockchain. The digital signature, or cryptographic keys are used to exchange money and secure contracts. Wei is believed by many to be Satoshi Nakamoto, nevertheless his paper was a call to action that was not met until Bitcoin came to be in 2008.

Note: The smallest unit of Ether (Ethereum) is called a Wei in honor of Wei Dai. Other denominations are Finney after Hal Finney, and Szabo after Nick Szabo, both of whom worked on cryptographic proof and cryptocurrency very early on. Also, both of whom along with Wei Dai are rumored as being Satoshi Nakamoto.

Essentially cryptocurrency is a medium of exchange that exists on a peer-to-peer network. The network works to secure transactions, oversee the creation of new monetary units and is cryptographically secured. The easiest definition for cryptocurrency is that it is digital cash, that is decentralized, fast, and secure. The internet is taking our day to day lives more and more into the digital realm. We socialize, learn, entertain ourselves, and shop on the internet. Digital cash is a necessity for how we live. As the digital lifestyle continues to grow the demand for fast, secure, and reliable digital cash will grow with it.

The current system of digital money consists of

electronic funds transfer (EFT) or wire transfer. A wire transfer usually occurs between banks or financial institutions using a network such as Swift or Fedwire. The process is secure and usually does not take any more than 3 days depending on the transaction type, many transactions being completed within a day. The procedure consists of funds being debited from your account and credited to another's account. This involves financial institutions as a central point of authority. EFT is how most transactions occur, a direct deposit from your employer for your wages is one example. Using a Debit/Credit card is also processed through EFT. The current system always involves at least one financial institution as a central point of authority and works on a ledger of credits and debits.

Cryptocurrency works much differently, money moves between the owners' wallets. There is no central point of authority, you are your own bank. The transaction processing is done by the miners and recorded on the public blockchain. Miners are rewarded for their efforts in verifying transactions and maintaining the blockchain. Incentivizing the miners adds another layer of security to the network. The ledger of credits and debits exists on the public blockchain. There is no wire transfer or EFT transaction, the transactions are completed as soon as they are verified by the miners and are mostly completed within minutes.

Some characteristics of cryptocurrency are pseudo-anonymity, borderless, secure, and trustless. To approve a cryptocurrency transaction a user must sign the transaction with their personal private cryptographic key. After the user verifies that they do want to continue with the transaction the wallet automatically signs the transaction with the users' private key. Pseudo-anonymity means that although you do not have to show identification for transactions, your transactions still go on the public blockchain. This means that you can be identified by your cryptographic key. This dispels one myth of cryptocurrency, that it is used by criminals because it is anonymous. Cryptocurrency can be spent anywhere from anywhere, it is borderless. Transactions can occur at any time 24 hours a day, 365 days a year. This is important for investors to know because unlike the stock market, cryptocurrencies trade 24 hours a day and on weekends.

Trust is an issue with paper currency, in our current system we trust institutions with our wealth. Institutions like governments who debase our currency, or banks who charge us for their trust. Cryptos are secure and trustless, they are secured by cryptography and the trust is distributed throughout the network. Cryptocurrency gives each individual holder the power of control over their own wealth. For the first time in human history, the power is taken from the few and given to the many. I believe this to be the biggest revolution that cryptocurrency is introducing.

Although Bitcoin was the first, there are many other cryptocurrencies now in circulation. The other cryptocurrencies are called alt coins, short for alternate coins. Some of the major ones introduced their own blockchain, these are referred to as coins. Other cryptocurrencies occupy or use existing blockchains and these are called tokens. Most of the coins are purposed as currency, some of the tokens are used as gas in their respective blockchains or are based on a developers' platform. The tokens serve as a means of exchange in the platforms, this is not to mean that they do not have value outside of the platform. There are many tokens that hold great value outside of their platform. For example, Maker (MKR) is a governance token of the Dai Stablecoin System, on the Ethereum blockchain, and it holds great value. At this time, I will be concentrating on the coins which carry their own blockchain.

Bitcoin (BTC)

Market Cap #1

Every informed person needs to know about Bitcoin because it might be one of the world's most important developments.

– Leon Luow

We have talked extensively about Bitcoin throughout the book, accordingly since Bitcoin is the mother of all cryptocurrencies. So, here I just want to hit the important aspects of Bitcoin and associate those aspects with the problems with fiat currency. Also, I want to highlight some of the problems Bitcoin introduced.

Bitcoin is a digital asset that enables peer-to-peer transactions without the need for a central authority. This is accomplished by use of Bitcoins two main components, the Bitcoin Token and the Bitcoin protocol. The token is what conveys value, it is the medium that allows value for value transactions. The protocol is a decentralized network that maintains a ledger of all the transactions of the token. Bitcoin is used to transact electronically, in this sense it is like conventional currencies such as the dollar, or the yen, but this is where the similarities end. To look at how it is different than fiat currency we need to bring back the problems with fiat currency to analyze.

Inflation and devaluation – As we discussed, conventional currency is devalued over time by central banks through monetary policy. Bitcoin avoids this by spreading the control of the currency throughout the entire system. It is maintained by miners who are incentivized to validate the transactions in the system. Bitcoin runs on an open network of dedicated computers spread out around the world.

Bitcoin has a limited supply, there will only ever be 21 million Bitcoin created. This is a counter-inflation mechanism. The supply of Bitcoin will always be the same meanwhile demand will increase over time which will make the value go up, along with your spending power. Essentially there is no central authority to devalue Bitcoin, and the limited supply will ensure that your spending power increases over time.

Locally based – Bitcoin is digital, which means it can be spent anywhere there is an internet connection. If the network can be reached Bitcoin can be spent. There are no borders, it is completely global. A person in Georgia can pay a writer from Sweden for his book over the internet using Bitcoin, all from the comfort of his couch.

No privacy – Bitcoin is pseudonymous, meaning that it is not completely anonymous. There are no names or identification cards required for transactions to occur. When a transaction goes to the miners for verification or to the blockchain to be recorded on the ledger, neither your name nor the other party's name is ever mentioned. The pseudo comes in because the transactions do contain a private key. The private key is used to verify transactions and can eventually be traced back to the source. So, when you sign for a transaction (use your private key) you are semi-anonymous in that your name is not associated. If someone really wanted to know they could trace the transaction back to you. The blockchain is public and anyone can view any transaction on the ledger.

Banks, not you, safeguard your money – This is a hotly debated subject, many people do not understand that when you get into crypto you are essentially becoming your own bank. Bitcoin takes the power of control away from institutions like banks, credit unions, and the government and puts it where it belongs, in your hands. That means that each individual person is responsible for the security of their funds. This entails some effort in learning how to safely transact in Bitcoin and other cryptocurrencies, and how to secure your currencies. A wallet secures your cryptocurrencies and it is also the means that allows you to interact with the blockchain. We will discuss wallets and how to safely transact with cryptocurrency in chapter 8 "How to Secure your Cryptocurrency".

Theft – Theft cannot be prevented, there will always be people who will steal what they can. Whenever there is an asset that has value there will be someone trying to steal it. The good news is that if you are smart about how you secure your cryptocurrency then you can be confident that your wealth is safe. Bitcoin, and cryptocurrency, in general, is safer or more secure than paper money. The cryptography associated with cryptocurrency ensures this. Carelessness in password selection or securing of cryptographic keys account for the main causes of theft in the system. If you are careful with your passwords and ensuring that your cryptographic keys are secured, then your cryptocurrencies will be safe.

Counterfeiting – Counterfeiting is an issue with paper money, such that the design and printing of money have changed many times over. Watermarks, embedded strips, raised lettering, holographic images, and color changing ink have been used to discourage counterfeiting of paper money. An issue that arose in early iterations of digital currency is "double spending".

Double spending is when the digital asset is copied and used more than once, essentially counterfeiting. This issue is solved with the use of cryptographic keys and the distributed ledger on the public blockchain. All this is handled by the miners who are incentivized to verify all the previous transactions on the blockchain. Every Bitcoin, whole or partial, is traceable to the very inception of it on the blockchain, thereby never having the ability to be double spent.

Bitcoin is also immutable, it is not reversible. There is no central authority or arbiter who can reverse a transaction. Once a transaction hits the network it is impossible to modify. You must be sure to double check before you spend on the Bitcoin network, once you sign the transaction and send it to miners for validation, you have less than an hour to change or reverse it. Once it is validated and hits the blockchain it cannot be changed.

Another advantage Bitcoin introduced is that it is divisible. In the stock market, it is impossible to buy a portion of a share of a company. Fractional shares can only be purchased in Dividend Reinvestment Plans (DRIP), which are only offered by certain corporations. There is no other way to purchase fractions of a share. The smallest denomination of Bitcoin is the Satoshi, it is one hundred millionth of a Bitcoin (0.00000001). Say

Bitcoin was trading at $8,000, then 100,000 Satoshi's, Sat's for short, would be $8. This means that you can buy less than one Bitcoin. For example, you could start buying Bitcoin on exchanges with small amounts of money and let it accumulate. This is what I did with Ether, and let it slowly accumulate, it makes it easier to get started.

Bitcoin lowers the barriers to entry in traditional investments, more people can get into the market because the divisibility means the cost is not prohibitive. Bitcoin introduced a new way of exchange, forever changing the financial landscape of the global economy. The public will now have control over their own money, with full autonomy to do with it as they please and safeguard it as they choose. All this while making transactions more secure and immutable, and making it globally available and spendable. Bitcoin tackled every problem with fiat currency and exceeded its expectations, yet it is not the final solution.

Along with innovation comes growing pains. Bitcoin introduced many new problems to tackle. Some of the problems Bitcoin has introduced are highlighted below:

Steep learning curve – Bitcoin can be difficult to get into. When you change how people have done something for centuries conversion will take time. Learning how to 'Crypto' can be daunting. Learning how to buy it, spend it, store it, and secure it will be difficult for some people. It is very technical indeed, and for older people, it could seem impossible. For most people who have adjusted to the internet, Facebook, Twitter, shopping on Amazon, etc. it will not be that difficult. There is a growing community who are trying to spread knowledge and allow the public to get started. This book is one of those efforts. Once you learn how to get into the market it is easier to use than traditional money.

Scalability – For Bitcoin or any other cryptocurrency to replace fiat currency, it must be liquid. Transactions must process quickly for Bitcoin to become a legit currency. When Bitcoin was released, the blocks on the blockchain could not be more than 1 megabyte (MB) to prevent spam. With a block taking approximately 10 minutes to build it only allows for a certain amount of transactions. For comparison Visa handles about 2,000 transactions per second (tps), Paypal handles around 115 tps, Bitcoin is currently around 7. This is a major disparity that will prevent mass adoption.

Impractical for Retail – As we see above Bitcoin is slow, this makes it difficult to conduct business on the Bitcoin network. The slowness of the system allows for some nefarious characters to double transact in the system. Once paying for the product and once paying themselves the Bitcoin back. Getting the product for free, essentially double spending. Retailers are having to turn to third-party payment service providers such as bitpay (www.bitpay.com) to handle transaction processing and to fix the double spending issue. This is inconvenient for retailers and flies in the face of what Bitcoin stands for, getting rid of third-party interference.

Although Bitcoin is the oldest of the cryptocurrencies and is already 10 years old, the cryptocurrency market is in its infancy. The innovation that cryptocurrency introduces is settling, growing, and maturing. There were many evolutions in the progression and maturation of the personal computer. Back in the 1970's, when computers filled an entire room, no one imagined that one day most everyone on the planet would be able to hold that same computational power in the palm of their hands. Innovations grow, mature, and change over time. Bitcoin will evolve, it will improve, and it will get better and easier to use.

There is a growing community of developers who are working on fixing the system. Some developers are taking what Bitcoin started and adding their own twist, at times to fix one or more of the issues above, other times to focus on other issues or concerns raised. Alternate coins, referred to as "Alt Coins", have come into existence to solve some of those problems, to create new systems, and innovate in this exciting new market.

Ethereum (ETH)

Market Cap #2

Ethereum has taken what was a four-function calculator of a programming language in Bitcoin and turned it into a full-fledged computer.

– Fred Ehrsam

Ethereum is the second largest cryptocurrency by market cap and the second most transacted cryptocurrency in the world. Ethereum, the brainchild of Vitalik Buterin, was first proposed in 2013. After a crowd-sale in 2014, the system went live on 30, July 2015. Ethereum is an open source, public blockchain and its goal is to provide the operating system in which developers can create blockchain projects using their smart contracts (scripting) technology. Essentially the Ethereum blockchain provides developers the ability to innovate new use cases for the blockchain. Some of these may be new cryptocurrencies and others may be something like a Decentralized Autonomous Organization (DAO, more on this later). Ethereum is a programmable blockchain, at the heart of it is the Ethereum Virtual Machine (EVM). The EVM is a Turing Complete suite that allows developers to create applications that run on the blockchain. Turing Complete means that it supports many different programing languages, making it more accessible.

Ethereum is leading the way for innovation in the blockchain community. The major innovation comes in the form of smart contracts. Smart contracts are self-executing assets where the terms of a contract are directly written into lines of code. Essentially these are programs in which parties can agree and ratify a transaction. These contracts are enforceable and legally binding as they exist on the distributed and decentral-ized blockchain. This introduces a revolutionary way of conducting business, digitizing contracts and removing unwanted third parties to ensure that business can be conducted only by the parties of concern.

The DAO

It's clear to me now that Ethereum is the new currency of the Internet. It's way ahead of where Paypal was in its day, and it's much more exciting to its customers than Paypal ever was.

– Gil Penchina

A DAO is an organization that can be programmed via smart contracts to run forever without the need for human interaction. The concept of the DAO was first brought to light in an article by Daniel Larimer in 2013. A DAO or DAC (Decentralized Autonomous Corporation) is a series of smart contracts that set the rules of how an organization will run. The idea is that people would buy into the DAO via tokens, the tokens would give the people voting rights. People would then vote on the direction of the organization. This is one example of the potential of the Ethereum blockchain with the use of the smart contracts.

Imagine companies without CEO's or any kind of hierarchy, instead being guided by the people who own the tokens. Although shareholders have voting rights in modern corporations, the direction of the company is still completely and autonomously controlled by the CEO and the board of directors. In a DAO there is no board, and no CEO, the organization cannot operate outside of the rules set forth in the programming (smart contracts). The organization is fully autonomous and guided by the owners, the token holders. The possibilities are limitless, imagine a ride share or cab company being run by a DAO. A fleet of driverless cars, picking people up collecting the fares, going to a recharge station to refuel, then moving on to the next fare, all run by the DAO's programming and guided by the token holders.

The first iteration of a DAO was an investor-directed venture capital fund called the DAO. The DAO was crowdfunded via a token sale in 2016 and set the record for the largest campaign in history. Unfortunately, the DAO was short-lived. It ran into some difficulties as weaknesses in the system were exploited by users to siphon off $50 million worth of Ethereum. It can be difficult to change the code once it is deployed on the blockchain, which is good because no one person can control or change the system, but bad in the fact that bugs existing in the system can go unchecked and possibly be exploited. This is what happened to the DAO, some users took advantage of the bugs to operate completely within the rules and siphon off the Ethereum.

A contentious decision was made to hard fork Ethereum in June 2016, for the purposes of returning the funds to the network. Immutability is very important in cryptocurrency. It is what prevents the developers or anyone for that matter, from changing something in the system for their own benefit. When a mistake is discovered in the programming it is near impossible to change because of the immutability. A hard fork means that a change is needed in the system and to accomplish this change the blockchain must fork into a new blockchain. The Ethereum hard fork created the modern day Ethereum network and cryptocurrency (ETH), the old Ethereum network still exists and is now Ethereum Classic (ETC). The dream of the DAO is still alive in the form of the cryptocurrency DASH, the Maker Stable Coin System, and digix.global.

Ethereum Classic (ETC)

I generally support just about every secession attempt that comes along. If, in the future, there is that kind of a dispute in Ethereum, I'd definitely be quite happy to see Ethereum A go in one direction and Ethereum B go the other.

– Vitalik Buterin

The Ethereum network cannot be blamed for the DAO disaster. As Gavin Wood (co-founder of Ethereum) put it blaming Ethereum for the DAO hack is like blaming the internet every time a website goes down. The Ether that was taken during the DAO hack was able to be recovered because of a rule (smart contract) that was put in place as a safeguard. The rule required people withdrawing from the DAO who got Ether in exchange for their DAO tokens, to retain the Ether in the system for 28 days. This gave the Ethereum community time to decide on how to unravel the DAO problem and recover the funds. This is where the community split, some people in the community did not want to do anything. Rationalizing that reversing the hacker's actions would go against the immutability of the blockchain which is what Ethereum stands for. The majority wanted a soft fork to fix the problem.

Think of a soft fork as a software update, the goal was to lock down the Ether the hacker stole to make it impossible for him to move. Although this was the popular choice it failed because doing this soft fork would expose the Ethereum network to hacker attacks which could bring down the entire system. The soft fork was a no go, the only way to fix the issue was to hard fork. A hard fork essentially breaks off the blockchain to create an entirely new blockchain. The decision to hard fork caused some discord amongst the Ethereum community, some members would not move to the new chain they remained on the old chain renaming it

Ethereum Classic (ETC). The new chain retained the name Ethereum and designated their coin ETH.

The difference between Ethereum (ETH) and Ethereum Classic (ETC) is the latter cannot access any updates from the Ethereum project. Ethereum Classic is not backward compatible, meaning that it chose not to transition to the new blockchain and it cannot access any of the upcoming updates of the Ethereum system. All the major players in the Ethereum community chose to transition to the new blockchain along with the original creators Vitalik Buterin, and Gavin Wood. One of the system updates that is coming, is a transition from proof of work to the up and coming proof of stake, more on this in the future.

I am a fan of the Ethereum network, it serves as the platform for many of the new coin offerings entering the market. The EVM is a great tool that is allowing developers to turn their dreams into reality, there are many projects in different stages of development, or that have already come out. Some carry their own token and others are applications on the blockchain that serve different purposes. The important factor is that they are all using the Ethereum blockchain and Ether is the gas in the system. This makes Ethereum is a great place to park your money in the cryptocurrency market.

Ripple (XRP)

Market Cap #3

[Bitcoin] is a remarkable cryptographic achievement... The ability to create something which is not duplicable in the digital world has enormous value...Lots of people will build businesses on top of that.

– Erik Schmidt

Ripple is different from other cryptocurrencies, in fact, it is not intended to be a currency. Ripple was made to provide a medium of fast exchange between different currencies. Ripple was created to bring the global payment infrastructure into the digital age. According to Ripple, RippleNet, the network by which Ripple seeks to connect the world's financial institutions is faster, more secure, and costs less than the current system. The plan is to sell the platform to financial institutions who need to transfer money in their day to day operations. The hope is that they will also use XRP along with the platform.

Ripple is a departure from what I have been professing all along this book. It is not a currency and there is a large amount of XRP in the system. Here is why I think Ripple is a great investment. Ripple is already announcing that deals have been completed with many financial institutions around the world, and there will be many more to come. When these institutions start using XRP it will burn those coins, meaning they will disappear from the network and never return. As of now, there are 500 Billion XRP coins. As Ripple makes more deals across the globe and financial institutions start burning all the XRP coins, the price per XRP will start rising.

Honorable Mentions

> *The reason we're all here is that the*
> *current financial system is outdated.*
>
> – Charlie Shrem

NEO (NEO) – Neo has been called the Chinese Ethereum, I like it because holding Neo gives a person free GAS tokens. Neo is the platform and Gas is the fuel for Neo's blockchain. Neo tokens held in one of the platform wallets (e.g. NEON Wallet) entitles the holder to Gas as a dividend for support of the Neo blockchain in block creation, network management, network creation, and other consensus requirements. Neo is a governance token and is indivisible, the lowest unit is 1 Neo. Gas is divisible and is used to pay fees in the blockchain for operations such as Digital Applica-tions (DApps), smart contracts, and incentivizing the maintenance of the blockchain. Neo is more established than the Waves network in DApp creation and support, it falls behind Ethereum in this sphere. The idea is the same as with Ethereum though, all the platforms being created on the Neo blockchain will ensure Neo and Gas will retain and grow in value in the future.

IOTA (MIOTA) – Iota is marketed as the Internet of Things blockchain. What is interesting is that Iota is completely reimagining the blockchain. Instead of blocks on a chain, Iota uses what they call a tangle. It represents a different way of thinking that may bring success in the future. Think of the blockchain as a straight line of transactions like an endless straight road, Iota is more like a cloud of transactions spreading in different directions like the branches of a tree. Every transaction in the cloud sprouts new transactions like a new bloom.

WAVES (WAVES) – Waves is another blockchain that is trying to compete with Ethereum in the DApp market. This is another way to make dividends like Neo provides. Waves is a Proof of Stake (PoS) platform. In the platform, a Waves holder can lease out their Waves to a PoS miner who in turn pays dividends to the token holder in the form of Waves and WavesGo tokens. We will dive into proof of stake further in the future but essentially stakers (miner equivalents in PoS systems) must own a lot of coins which they then

'stake' for the opportunity to collect fees by maintaining the blockchain and verifying transactions. Waves'
innovation is the ability to lease your coins to a staker
for a portion of the fees collected.

Litecoin (LTC) - Litecoin is a peer-to-peer cryptographically secure decentralized digital currency.
It is the brainchild of Charlie Lee, a former Google
employee. The Litecoin network is nearly identical to
Bitcoin, and it markets itself as the "Silver" to Bitcoins'
"Gold". Litecoin's objective is to be a lightweight
alternative to Bitcoin. Among the few differences in
Litecoin is faster block generation, 2.5 minutes as
opposed to Bitcoins 10 minutes. Litecoin also uses
script (Ethereum) instead of SHA-256 (Bitcoin) as
a hashing algorithm. Since its inception, Litecoin has
consistently been in the top 10 cryptocurrencies by
market cap. There are mixed opinions about Litecoin,
my advice if you want to invest go to the source to
research it.

Stellar Lumens (XLM) – Stellar aims to provide
more liquidity between currencies. It works on
consensus algorithm as opposed to mining making it
faster than most cryptocurrencies. The objective is to
provide a seamless system for low-cost transactions
to occur in and between any currency whether crypto

or fiat, in a peer-to-peer system or through financial institutions. Stellar is a non-stock non-profit organization whose mission it is to connect people to low-cost financial services to fight poverty and maximize individual potential.

Full disclosure, I do own some of these currencies. I would not want people to think that I am only mentioning what I own. I am a big believer in Ethereum, and I do own ETH. I believe the Ethereum project is changing the game with their smart contract technology. I own some Neo and Waves, mostly because I wanted to experience the dividend investing capability of these two platforms. I also own Ripple. I do not own IOTA nor Litecoin. Litecoin is not for me but could be a good investment for other people. It is imperative that you do your own research and see what you connect with. Although I do not own any at this time I think Stellar Lumens is a very interesting project that could have some very good upside.

There are other cryptos out there that would make for good investments, here are a few that I like and have researched: Monero, Dash, EOS, Cardano. Do your own research and see which projects make sense to you. Some of these are very good ventures and some have the potential to take off. There are many cryptocurrencies out now and more coming every day, the vast majority are scams and will die out eventually. It is of the utmost importance that you conduct thorough research into any investment you plan to make. Weed out the bad apples to find the diamond(s) in the rough.

CHAPTER 7

HOW TO BUY CRYPTOCURRENCY

There may be other currencies like it that may be even better. But in the meantime, there's a big industry around Bitcoin.—People have made fortunes off Bitcoin, some have lost money. It is volatile, but people make money off of volatility too.

– Richard Branson

As we have seen there are several good reasons to invest in cryptocurrency. One reason to invest is to hedge your wealth against the fall of the fiat currencies. Another is to support the social vision of cryptocurrencies one global, secure, and decentralized currency, with privacy and freedom for all. Finally, because you understand and want to support the technological innovations cryptocurrency has brought forth. A bad reason to invest is fear of missing out (FOMO), rushing into the market and buying at the top without first understanding cryptocurrency. As we have learned, you must understand the tools you are using to build wealth.

Do not invest in anything without first understanding and researching what you are buying and how it will return wealth to you.

Buying cryptocurrency can be difficult, it is different from anything that currently exists. It is not like buying stocks or bonds. The first step to buying cryptocurrency is to join an exchange. Some exchanges require you to prove your identity others are simpler to join. When you first join an exchange do not be alarmed by the amount of information they require from you. KYC means Know Your Customer, this is a requirement for more and more exchanges, it is a process by which the exchange authorities verify your identity. AML means Anti Money Laundering, this is a protocol by which authorities verify you are not a criminal intending to hide criminal activities by laundering money through crypto-assets. KYC and AML represent attempts by governmental agencies to gain some form of control over the cryptocurrency market and can sometimes interfere with the growth of the system.

Another way of buying cryptocurrency is through the developers of an ICO, you can buy directly from them during their presale. This is more a speculative investment and you must be knowledgeable about cryptocurrency to use this strategy. That said, here I will focus more on the established currencies through an exchange. If through research you do find an ICO you may want to be a part of or invest in, by-all-means go for it. Follow the guidelines we discussed earlier, ensure currency has a limited supply, research the team, ensure the projects have good use cases, see if the project solves a problem, finally ensure you will be able to liquidate (will they eventually be listed on an exchange). One issue in the ICO space is that most are not offered in all areas. For example, the United States government has been looking to regulate ICO offerings which has caused many developers to exclude U.S. citizens from their offerings. There are workarounds for this, but you must be careful in how you proceed. ICO's offer excellent avenues to get in on the ground floor of most projects. As such they should not be dismissed, but a bit of caution and extreme vetting is needed if this is a path that interests you.

Exchanges

*The stock market clearly values companies
that can deliver disruptive innovation.*

– Steve Blank

Exchanges are marketplaces where products are bought and sold. These products can be stocks, bonds, commodities, cryptocurrencies, and any other financial instrument. Exchanges provide a stable environment for trading activities along with efficient price dissemination. They do this by providing liquidity in the market. Market liquidity is a feature that allows products to be bought and sold quickly without greatly affecting price (stability). In highly liquid markets products can be bought and sold quickly with little impact on price. Most markets are centralized, meaning there is one single point of authority who provides all these functions. Examples of centralized exchanges are the New York Stock Exchange (NYSE), the Chicago Mercantile Exchange (CME), London Stock Exchange (LSE), Tokyo Stock Exchange (JPX), and the fiat currency market the FOREX (FX).

There are different types of exchanges for cryptocurrency, centralized and decentralized. Centralized exchanges are the more established of the two. The exchange serves as the central authority through which all transactions are conducted. The cryptocurrency is still decentralized but you are buying it in a central- ized exchange. Decentralized exchanges have started rising in popularity of late. They have been made possible by the introduction of smart contracts thanks to the Ethereum project. A decentralized exchange is one where investors can trade in cryptocurrency with other investors in a peer to peer network without a central authority. Decentralized exchanges are very new, they currently work on unproven technology, although growing in popularity very quickly. The decentralized nature of cryptocurrency begs for the operability of a decentralized vehicle of exchange. Decentralized exchanges will eventually become the preferred method of buying and selling cryptocurrency.

Characteristics of a Centralized Exchange

I think the internet is going to be one of the major forces for reducing the role of government. The one thing that's missing but that will soon be developed is a reliable e-cash.

– Milton Friedman

In a centralized exchange, there is a trusted middleman, a central authority, that facilitates the trading of products on their platform. The exchange handles trading by providing the trade book, the trade book is where all the information about the sellers and buyers of a product is kept. The exchange matches sellers and buyers in the trade book to complete the trading transactions. The matching is conducted through trading algorithms. The software matches the sellers with buyers at a determined price or a market price. Since there is a central authority involved in the trade the sellers must keep their products in the system to be able to sell them on the platform. This also means that the buyer does not actually possess or own the coins until they are withdrawn from the exchange. Until the assets are withdrawn they only exist in the database as a credit to the investor from the exchange. This ensures the exchange will continue to provide liquidity in the asset which enables price stability of said asset.

There are different types of orders an investor can make. A general order where the investor does not want to buy or sell at a specific price is called a market order. In a market order, the buy or sell order will be filled at the current market price. Limit orders allow buyers and sellers to set the price terms while setting up their trade. For example, a trader wants to buy 10 NEO and is not willing to pay more than $50 per coin, the system would then match the buyer with a seller who is willing to sell their coins for $50 per coin or less.

This central point of authority exposes the central exchanges to several hazards. The central authorities of the exchange can be subjected to government influence. For example, a government can impose unilateral restrictions on the exchange in an effort to control cryptocurrency under the guise of protecting consumers. A central point of control also exposes the exchange to hacker attacks. Since investors must keep their assets in the system to trade them this exposes their assets to hackers. Centralized exchanges are built by companies interested in making profits, they make these profits by charging fees for transactions in the system. These fees can get expensive and cumbersome to high volume traders.

Another issue with central exchanges is they limit

or cap withdrawals. The exchange is providing the liquidity for the market, and as such cannot allow a massive exodus of investors from the exchange. To solve this issue, they put restrictions on the amount an individual investor can take out of the market. With the massive flood of investors coming into the crypto market some exchanges have had to restrict new sign-ups and have had to shut down at times to upgrade the software. These issues have created an opportunity cost problem for some investors who cannot trade while the exchange is shut down. This recently happened where an exchange shut down for what was meant to be four hours, four days later the exchange was still closed, meanwhile, the market was in a downturn. People were not able to access their assets to sell, trade, or even buy on the dip.

Along with the bad aspects of centralized exchanges there is also good aspects. The central exchanges make it easier to get into the market by providing the platform for new investors to get started. Access to the platforms is more familiar to the common investor. They use tools such as account numbers, passwords, and/or pins. They provide liquidity to the market, and they are starting to offer leveraged and margin trading. Limit orders are also a bonus of centralized exchanges. Although trading directly in peer-to-peer fashion could be considered limit ordering because the seller and buyer are coming to an agreement on price. It is also important to note that centralized exchanges offer fiat to cryptocurrency exchange, which is still beyond the scope of decentralized exchanges. Some of the more popular central exchanges:

Centralized Exchanges

- Coinbase (Fiat trade pairs available)
- Binance (Soon to have fiat trade pairs)
- Bittrex
- Kraken
- Bitmex (Leveraged Trading)
- Coinsetter (Fiat trade pairs available)
- Cryptsy (Fiat deposits available)
- Bitstamp
- BTC-e (Wall Street Grade Technology)

Characteristics of a Decentralized Exchange (DEX)

At its core, bitcoin is a smart currency, designed by very forward-thinking engineers. It eliminates the need for banks, gets rid of credit card fees, currency exchange fees, money transfer fees, and reduces the need for lawyers in transactions… all good things.

– Peter Diamandis

The smart contract innovations brought on by Ethereum introduced the means to start thinking about decentralized exchanges. The first of these types were built on the Ethereum blockchain (Etherdelta, and later Airswap, and Raiden). These exchanges can only handle ERC-20 tokens which is the Ethereum standard. As is common innovation breeds innovation, now there are other decentralized exchanges which are being built with their own blockchain which essentially works as a transaction layer sitting on top of other blockchains. This is a little technical, suffice it to say these new decentralized exchanges are blockchain agnostic. Blockchain agnostic means that they can transact on any blockchain. This means that these new decentralized exchanges can transact in many different cryptocurrencies regardless of which blockchain the tokens use. This is made possible by an innovation called an Atomic Swap. Atomic swaps allow users to trade any cryptocurrency for any other without the need of a trusted third party. Essentially atomic swaps remove the trust problem in trading cryptocurrencies.

Decentralized exchanges remove the need of a central controlling authority, they provide the means for peer-to-peer transactions. They serve as a matching and routing layer for trade orders and run on a distributed ledger system. Removing the central authority solves the security issues of central exchanges. The exchange cannot be pressured by any government to enforce unwanted restrictions. The same secure technology of the distributed ledger, featured on the blockchain, is used by DEX's which detracts hackers from trying to attack the exchange. Since there is no central point of control and information that hackers can hone in on.

Transactions in a decentralized exchange happen from an investor's private wallet, there is no need to keep any assets on the exchange. Trading this way ensures more privacy for the investors. This raises an issue of liquidity, in traditional markets liquidity is provided by the exchange who keep assets on deposit. In decentralized exchanges this is not the case, the result is more volatility in price movement on these exchanges. Some newer exchanges have started providing liquidity by maintaining a certain amount of the most common assets such as Bitcoin or Ethereum. By doing this the exchanges can maintain better control over prices. Decentralized exchanges charge lower fees than traditional exchanges. The fees incurred are for interacting with the blockchain only (mining fees, staking fees), the exchange fees are minimal, some exchanges do not charge fees. Users trade directly from their wallets, the fees incurred are mostly transaction processing fees which can accumulate yet are still a great deal less than centralized exchange fees.

Although the decentralization of the exchanges solves many problems of centralized exchanges they do have their limitations as well. The main detractor of decentralized exchanges is the user interface. The user interface is clunky and difficult to use for a layman. Some newer exchanges are tackling these issues with interfaces that are more familiar to traders and investors. Another issue is the types of trades allowed by the exchanges. For example, limit and stop loss trades. As the technology advances fiat trade pairs will become more common. Currently, access to cryptocurrency via fiat currency is not available. This means that investors will have to convert fiat currency into cryptocurrency via centralized exchanges when starting out.

Most of the issues with decentralized exchanges are

being tackled through innovation in the space. Radar Relay, for example, is testing their system for limit orders with stop loss capabilities. OmiseGo is working on providing fiat trade pairs. Meanwhile, Herdius and Block DX are working on cross blockchain trading to provide the ability for users to trade any cryptocurrency pairs. Some of the most popular decentralized exchanges are listed below:

Decentralized Exchanges

- IDEX (ERC-20 Tokens)
- WAVES DEX (BTC, ETH, and Waves Tokens)
- OpenLedger (Multiple Currencies)
- Radar Relay (ERC-20 Tokens)
- Stellar DEX (Few Currencies)
- Block DX (Blockchain agnostic, in development)
- OmiseGo (Fiat, ERC-20 Tokens)
- Oasis DEX (ERC-20 Tokens)
- Herdius (Blockchain agnostic, in development)

Getting Started

The first panacea for a mismanaged nation is inflation of the currency; the second is war. Both bring a temporary prosperity; both bring a permanent ruin. But both are the refuge of political and economic opportunists.

– Ernest Hemingway

When I started in the crypto markets I did not have the knowledge base I have now, and you will have from this book. I started on Coinbase, for people in the U.S. it is one option where you can deposit dollars. Other options include Kraken and Gemini. Typically, you will need to verify your account, usually by providing your driver's license or passport. This is done via the camera on your computer. First taking pictures of your face then of your identifying documents. Coinbase offers deposits straight from a bank account, via wire transfer, ACH transfer, or a credit card purchase. As you verify your identity and connect a payment system your purchase and withdrawal limit will rise.

There are two different systems an investor can access on Coinbase. One is Coinbase where you can link an account and purchase Ethereum (ETH), Bitcoin (BTC), Bitcoin Cash (BCH), and Litecoin (LTC). The second is the GDAX which is laid out more like a traditional exchange where you can purchase and trade these currencies. If you use the GDAX plan on deposits taking 5 to 7 business days to process, wire transfers are somewhat faster. Once the money is deposited into the GDAX then trading is enabled. On Coinbase, you can link your account and purchase directly from your account, which means you can lock in the price when you purchase. Once you purchase on Coinbase it will take 5 to 7 business days for the coins to be available in the Coinbase wallet. Important note to remember is that all these currencies are divisible. This means that you don't have to wait until you have enough to purchase one whole coin, you can buy a part of a coin.

For people outside the U.S. there are other options which may be easier to access in your native currency. For Australia, BTC Markets is the best option, for Korea Bitthumb or Coinone, and for Canada QuadrigaCX. Most centralized exchanges are available to Europeans with the most popular being Coinbase, HitBTC, and Kraken. Some African countries have had some major issues with their central banks, the history there reads like a horror script. For Africans there are many options, some of the more popular ones are Bitmari, Bitpesa, Geopay, Naira Exchange, and Kobocoin. Central and South America have had similar tough sledding with some depressed economies and many devalued currencies. In Central and South America Coinmama, MexBT, and Bitex offer crypto exchange services. Once the fiat is converted into crypto it becomes borderless and can be moved to any cryptocurrency exchange to be traded or used as currency.

Once you have converted your fiat to cryptocurrency it is advisable to move the cryptocurrency off of the exchange wallet. Exchanges are susceptible to hacker attacks and are targets for government regulation, either will put your assets at risk. If trading is your goal, moving assets in and out of exchanges is fairly easy. Some good exchanges for trading are Binance, Bittrex, Poloniex, and Kraken. There are others which show some promise, just as we do our research on what to purchase for investment you must also do your research on where you invest as well. The fee schedule is unique to each exchange, the features offered are different and unique as well.

Everything is done through digital wallets; these wallets give the users public and private keys. These keys are long alphanumeric strings that serve as wallet addresses. When you register for a wallet you will be given a private and a public key. Keep your private key secure, never share it, when you spend cryptocurrency your private key is automatically attached to the transaction as your signature of approval. The public key serves as the public address of your wallet, it is how cryptocurrency gets transferred to your wallet. When you spend or transfer cryptocurrency you will send the assets to the receivers' public key, their public address.

Different wallets will have different user interfaces, but they will all have a way to transfer funds. When you transfer funds, you will enter the receiving address in the box that says enter receiving address. You can accomplish this through copy and pasting the address, scanning a QR code, or by inputting the address manually. Whichever you choose you must ensure to double check to ensure it is the correct address. Ethereum addresses will always start with 0x if they show something other than that it is not an Ethereum address. When you click on these addresses it will take you to Etherscan (www.etherscan.io). On Etherscan you can verify the address to ensure it is not a scammer. Etherscan provides access to the Ethereum blockchain where you can check the addresses activities, transactions, contracts, etc. Next, we will dive deeper into how to secure your cryptocurrency and how to use wallets.

CHAPTER 8

HOW TO SECURE CRYPTOCURRENCY

Bitcoin will do to banks what email did to the postal industry.
– Rick Falkvinge

Many people do not realize that cryptocurrency is a complete change from the way we have traditionally done things in the financial sphere. There is no institution looking out for you, security is now every individuals' personal responsibility. Banks have traditionally assumed the role of safeguarding people's wealth for which they charge hefty fees. Cryptocurrency allows each person to become their own bank. With this new responsibility of safeguarding your own money comes many issues you must be aware of. How to protect your money from theft, how to transfer money safely, and how to transact safely. In the crypto world, all this happens with the use of digital wallets.

Digital wallets provide cryptocurrency owners with access to the blockchain. They are computer programs that allow users to interface and transact with the blockchain. You will transact with the blockchain of the cryptocurrency of your choice, by way of your digital wallet. Before we continue, we must understand how this all works. There is no physical form of cryptocurrency, the wallet does not actually contain any digital currency. There are no physical coins anywhere, nor does a digital wallet contain any currency, digital or otherwise. The digital wallet only contains a public and private key. The currency exists on the blockchain through the recorded transactions on the public ledger. Ownership of the cryptocurrency is tied to your public and private keys.

Clear are mud, ok let's continue. The one thing to understand from all this is that your private key is to be safeguarded at all costs. All the other stuff is a little technical and only provides a backdrop for understanding how digital wallets work. Something else we must understand is that wallets only support certain kinds of cryptocurrencies. For example, there are wallets which only support one kind of currency, there are others which support multiple currencies. It is important to know what currencies are supported by the wallet you are researching.

There are two classifications of wallets, hot and

cold. A hot wallet is one that is connected to the internet and as such is vulnerable to attacks. A cold wallet is the safest option, it is rarely connected to the internet and as such less vulnerable to attacks. There are different reasons to choose the different classes of wallets. For example, if you want the convenience of having your funds available to you immediately then a hot wallet should be your choice. If you are holding a large amount of currency as an investment for the long term, then maybe a cold storage wallet would be a better choice. Along with the different classes of wallets, there are also different types of wallets. Online, desktop, hardware, and paper wallets are the different types of wallets. The different types of wallets can be either hot or cold, sometimes both. All this can be very confusing, especially to someone just starting out, to clarify let's break it down even further.

Hot Wallets

Online Wallet – Ultimate convenience, lowest security. Wallets run on the cloud and are accessible from anywhere there is an internet connection. Keys are stored online usually by a third party which makes them vulnerable to hacking attacks. Exchanges such as Coinbase and Binance have online wallets. Jaxx wallet is another example of an online wallet, it is also a mobile wallet. Jaxx is highly regarded for its ease of use, and because it allows for storage of multiple currencies. I personally use the Jaxx wallet and do recommend it for smaller amounts, as my investment in crypto is growing I am looking to move to more secure means of storage. Some of the top online wallets:

- Jaxx

- Exodus

- Metamask

- MyEtherWallet

Mobile Wallet - Very self-explanatory, these wallets run on an app on your phone. They are usually much simpler than other types of wallets. Security is low for this kind of wallet. Some of the top mobile wallets:

- MyCelium

- BreadWallet

- Jaxx

Desktop Wallet – Desktop wallets are more secure than their online or mobile counterparts. Desktop wallets are downloaded to a computer and only exist on that computer. However, if the computer gets a virus or is hacked then all funds could be lost. A good way to avoid loss is to back-up the public and private keys with cold storage, this is as simple as writing them down on a piece of paper and storing the paper somewhere safe. Another concern with desktop wallets is whether they are available in Windows, Mac, or Linux. Some of the top desktop wallets:

- Exodus
- mSIGNA
- Copay

Cold Wallets

Hardware Wallet – Hardware wallets store private keys on pluggable USB type devices. A user can simply plug in the device to an internet connected device, enter a pin, complete their transactions, then unplug the device. The fact that the private keys are stored offline makes them more secure than hot wallets. It is important to note that when you have your device plugged into an internet-connected computer it is a hot wallet and susceptible to attack. If you are an investor and will not be transacting too much with cryptocurrency, then this is the type of wallet to get. Also, if you start accumulating a large stack then I would start looking at this type of wallet. Most hardware wallets support multiple currencies. The top hardware wallets are:

- Ledger Nano S
- Trezor Bitcoin Wallet
- KeepKey Bitcoin Wallet

Paper Wallets - Paper wallets can be as simple as physically writing down your public and private keys and putting them in your safe. Paper wallets can also be software programs that generate random keys which are then printed out and stored. Paper wallets represent the highest form of security because they are never plugged into the internet, just don't lose the paper.

Coinbase and other cryptocurrency exchanges have wallets associated with their platform. These are absolutely the least safe wallets around and represent the lowest form of storage. Coinbase has, so far, avoided hackers but all the other exchanges have been hacked at least once. If you have cryptocurrency on an exchange wallet it could be at risk if the exchange gets hacked. This is not to say that you should not use these exchanges or exchange wallets at all, they serve a purpose just like anything else. If you are a trader, the easiest way to do it and avoid transaction fees for transferring money from different wallets is to just keep your currency on the exchange wallet.

Core wallets are downloaded directly from the developers of the cryptocurrency. Core wallets can be used by developers to support applications on the blockchain and allow direct interaction with the blockchain. Core wallets are specific to that individual currency and any currency supported by that specific blockchain. Core wallets are, for the most part, online wallets and as such hot wallets. For example, the Ethereum Core wallet allows anyone to store Ether along with other ERC-20 currencies built on the Ethereum blockchain. It also allows for the creation, use, and deployment of smart contracts on the blockchain.

Different wallets work in different ways, the most popularly used practice is a passphrase. When you set up your wallet you will be asked to come up with a passphrase or you will be given a passphrase to remember. A passphrase is usually a series of 12 words, their purpose is to recover your wallet in case you forget your password. Keep your passphrase safe, and accessible, do not forget it or your access to the wallet may be lost along with your assets. Next, you will be asked to set up a password for your wallet. Access to the wallet is through your password, a strong password is essential.

Safe Wallet Practices

If privacy is outlawed, only outlaws will have privacy.
– Phil Zimmermann

Wallets will safeguard your currency and they are good tools to use to transact safely in the crypto world, but laziness or ignorance can void any wallets security protocol. There are safety practices we must get used to practicing. For example, weak passwords can be hacked easily and then your funds can disappear. So, here are some ideas to safeguard your cryptocurrency in the online world.

Obviously, the first security measure is creating strong passwords. One of the biggest problems in modern society is weak passwords. Weak passwords lead to stolen identity, runaway social media profiles, and theft. Make strong passwords for your wallets, and do not use the same password for every single application that you use regularly. There are software programs that will help you manage all these different passwords, use these to keep track of all your new passwords. Use safe practices for passwords, for example, do not use your kid's names or birthdates as your passwords.

Secondly, you must update your wallets software. Every day hackers are coming up with new ways to steal public and private keys. A new attack I found in which the hack changes the public key, when it is copied and pasted, to the hackers' key so they get the payment instead of who it was intended for. The updates ensure that your wallet is up to date to defend against all the latest and greatest hacker tactics. It is important to keep your computer software and wallet software up to date to ensure that you are protected from the latest attacks.

Other Security Measures

Man maintains his balance, poise, and sense of security
only as he is moving forward.

– Maxwell Maltz

The current online culture demands all of us to engage in safety practices to ensure our security. These practices should be adopted by all and at all times while working online. Hiding your head underground like an ostrich is not an option anymore, everything is online and not being online is backward and unproductive. To be online we must be security conscious. Some of the following tips are for general online security, some are for cryptocurrency in general, but all should be followed.

To operate online these days, you must protect yourself from all kinds of attacks. Information is the currency of the connected world. Hackers will come after you to try to gain access to your personal information through different attacks such as phishing, virus attacks, malware, keylogger, fake WAP, and many more. There are basic things one can do to protect against these threats. Some are simple and common-sense things like never enter your password or pin codes into an untrusted website or a site that does not have trusted certificates. Never fill out information forms unless it is a trusted site. Be very careful when downloading files online. Ensure that you know what you are downloading and that it comes from a trusted website. Practice safe browsing, surfing the internet is fun but ensure that you are steering toward good sites and stay away from bad sites, I think we all know what we're talking about here. Going to the museum or the zoo is great but stay away from the red-light district. Finally, make sure your internet connection is secure before entering personal information. Never enter account or personal information into a website while connected to a public Wi-Fi. If you are unsure whether the connection is secure it is better to wait until you are at home or at work where you can be sure of the secure connection.

Keep your antivirus software up to date and ensure that it includes a complete online suite. Antivirus software can be expensive but these days it is essential. Most antivirus software now includes online suites and most of these will warn you if you are going into dangerous online territory. The software will ensure that the sites you visit have trusted certificates. Trusted sites are where you are safe to enter personal information into forms and make safe online purchases. Antivirus software will also ensure that you are downloading safely by scanning your downloads before you unpack them. An antivirus suite will help secure your online experience and allow you to operate in the online world. To know you are on a secure server look at the address bar (where the website's name is) and ensure that it says HTTPS instead of HTTP. The antivirus will also show you if its secure by showing a closed lock icon before the address bar, making all or part of the address green, or by simply adding the word secure before the address.

Social media is a great outlet to exercise your creativity, let your voice be heard, express your opinions, or just check in with your friends and family. It is also a hotbed for hacker activity. Always be mindful of what you are putting up on social media website for the world to see. Do not ever post any personal information, anything that can be used to access your accounts or otherwise steal from you. In the military we called this operational security, meaning don't ever post anything that could put you or your family in danger. This extends to anything that could be used to steal from you, whether that be your accounts or your identity.

Metacert is an internet security program, they make browser extensions that will verify the websites you are visiting are secure. One such program is Cryptonite which is a web browser add-on that protects you against phishing scams and against fake Twitter profiles. When surfing the internet with the Cryptonite extension the software will check each site's certificate and will notify you if they are untrustworthy or dangerous. When a site is trustworthy the address in the address bar will be green, this notifies you that it is a trusted site and it is ok to proceed. Metacert is an excellent cyber-security company, their products are free and very easy to use even for a newbie.

Other security measures that are easy to use and very commonly used in the crypto world, are 2FA verification. This is to verify you are who you say you are and ensure that it is not someone trying to use your account. 2FA will send a code to your phone which you will then enter into the website you are trying to access. Google authenticator is another security and verifying program. Use your Google account to set up Google Authenticator and download the app. Websites will offer Google Authenticator for clients, once you access this feature on the website it will send a code to the app on your phone. The app will have time-limited codes for all the websites you have set up with the feature. You would then enter the code to access the site. For the leeriest people out there, random password generators are available online which will help you generate hyper secure passwords for your different accounts. RoboForm is a password manager provider, with their software you can setup all your logins under one master password. RoboForm is available for download on their website and works as a browser extension. They can help you secure all your logins and it works on multiple platforms. Although this software is available for free download you do have to pay for the services.

Note: I am in no way affiliated with nor compensated by any of the service providers mentioned above. I found them through research and they are only provided here as examples of service providers. It is always my advice to conduct your own research and find what works best for you and your family.

Being online is not an option anymore, the world is connected through the internet. Being connected means that you are risking your privacy. Protect yourself and your interests by using safety and security products and practicing safe surfing techniques. The identity theft statistics are daunting, according to the Identity Theft Resource Center (ITRC) the number of credit cards exposed to fraud was up 88 percent from 2016 to 2017. Also, 158 million Social Security Numbers were exposed in 2017, more than 8 times the amount seen in 2016. The importance of safeguarding your information cannot be overstated. Carelessly exposing yourself and your family online is dangerous and has severe consequences. Adopt the safe practices mentioned above to protect yourself and your family.

CHAPTER 9

GO FORTH AND CONQUER!

I always tell my family that the second most stupid thing they could do right now is to own an amount of bitcoins they cannot afford to lose, and the most stupid thing they could do would be to not own any.

– Wence Caceres, CEO Xapo

Someday consumers and businesses won't hold Bitcoins for their account but will unknowingly access the Bitcoin network whenever payments are made."

– Paul Vigna

We have taken a journey together, from the very beginning of trade through history to the digital age of currency. We have learned of the need for currency, as a store of value in exchange for goods. We saw how the current system is broken, the problems fiat currencies carry, and the solutions provided by cryptocurrency. We reviewed one idea of how to create an investment plan, the possibilities for investment plans are endless. You are only limited by your own creativity. We learned how to conduct research and where to start building your knowledge. We dove into the world of cryptocurrency and found the amazing innovation behind it, the blockchain. We learned about some of the most popular cryptocurrencies and their uses and potential. Finally, we learned how to get started buying crypto and how to secure it once you own it.

The technological advancements of the blockchain, the distributed ledger, and cryptocurrency will help advance humanity into the digital era. Thus far we have focused on how everyone can individually profit from this technological innovation, but there is so much more to come. The financial system is broken, the governmental system is broken, something must change. Humanity is facing some of the biggest problems it has ever faced with global warming, climate change, deforestation, hunger, resource exhaustion (particularly scary is fresh water), and poverty all threatening the success of our species. These technologies seek to create a new world, a united world. Currency is the first step in a long voyage to becoming a unified civilization as opposed to a divided squabbling group of nations that cannot agree on anything.

Imagine a world where we as a people can govern

ourselves. Instead of incessant bickering between lawmakers arguing over everything and never coming to a decision. We as a people could decide how to tackle all these issues facing humanity. The government itself is not broken, it's how we elect our governors that is a problem. The decentralized nature of the blockchain and the distributed ledger can allow us to reimagine the way we govern. Imagine being able to fix the problems our planet faces, being able to reverse global warming thereby ensuring that the one and only planet that we can live on will continue to support us. Imagine using all the worlds combined resources to find another earth and colonize space. The future is now, the community of developers and innovators are already working on all these issues. We as a civilization are now taking our first baby steps toward a united future.

The quote above from Paul Vigna points to the fact that this is still a very young market. I hinted that the cryptocurrency to replace all currency, the future global currency, may not have been created yet. I encourage everyone to dig deeper into this market and you will reap the benefits of this incredible opportunity. This book is a good first step but do not stop here, keep digging. There are new resources and opportunities every day and the more engaged you are with the community the easier it will be to spot the best ones and ride them to the top. This book is intended to be a manual, a good first step into the market. I hope it helps many people along their journey, and I hope you enjoyed it.